Your Guide to Energy Healing

Awakening the Healer Within provides answers to some of the most frequently asked questions about energy-based healing. What kind of techniques are available? Is healing temporary, or can energy-based healing techniques provide a permanent cure? What does a healer really do? Is healing a special gift for only a few, or can anyone learn to be a healer?

This easy-to-follow guide is your introduction to several energy-based healing techniques that have repeatedly demonstrated a positive effect on those who want to accelerate their healing process. Discover the origins of illness and disease, the five levels of the human energy field, and how to become a channel for healing at each level.

About the Author

Howard F. Batie, DM, is a retired naval officer and satellite communications engineer. He is now director of the Evergreen Healing Arts Center, his holistic healing practice in Chehalis, Washington. Howard teaches classes in energy-based healing for both professional and lay persons at a local two-year college. His website is www.localaccess.com/Healing-Hands.

To Write to the Author

If you wish to contact the author or would like more information about this book, please write to the author in care of Llewellyn Worldwide and we will forward your request. Both the author and publisher appreciate hearing from you and learning of your enjoyment of this book and how it has helped you. Llewellyn Worldwide cannot guarantee that every letter written to the author can be answered, but all will be forwarded. Please write to:

Howard F. Batie
% Llewellyn Worldwide
P.O. Box 64383, Dept. K055-8
St. Paul, MN 55164-0383, U.S.A.
Please enclose a self-addressed stamped envelope for reply,
or $1.00 to cover costs. If outside U.S.A., enclose
international postal reply coupon.

Many of Llewellyn's authors have websites with additional information and resources. For more information, please visit our website at www.llewellyn.com.

An Introduction to Energy-Based Techniques

Awakening

the

Healer

Within

Howard F. Batie, DM

2000
Llewellyn Publications
St. Paul, Minnesota 55164-0383, U.S.A.

615.89
BATIE

First Edition
First Printing, 2000

Book design and editing by Michael Maupin
Cover design by Anne-Marie Garrison
Interior illustrations by Carrie Westfall

Ro-Hun[SM] is a service mark of Ro-Hun Institute, McCaysville, GA.

Library of Congress Cataloging-in-Publication Data
Batie, Howard F. (Howard Franklin), 1939 –
    Awakening the healer within : an introduction to energy-based techniques /
        Howard F. Batie.
        p.   cm.
    Includes bibliographical references and index.
    ISBN: 1-56718-055-8
    1. Vital force—Therapeutic use. 2. Mental healing. I. Title.
RZ999.B28   2000
615.8'9—dc21   00-058484

Llewellyn Worldwide does not participate in, endorse, or have any authority or responsibility concerning private business transactions between our authors and the public.

All mail addressed to the author is forwarded but the publisher cannot, unless specifically instructed by the author, give out an address or phone number.

Note: The practices, techniques, and meditations described in this book should *not* be used as an alternative to professional medical treatment. This book does not attempt to give any medical diagnosis, treatment, prescription, or suggestion for medication in relation to any human disease, pain, injury, deformity, or physical condition.

The author and publisher of this book are not responsible in any manner whatsoever for any injury which may occur through following the instructions contained herein. It is recommended that before beginning any alternative healing practice you consult with your physician to determine whether you are medically, physically, and mentally fit to undertake the practice.

Llewellyn Publications
A Division of Llewellyn Worldwide, Ltd.
P.O. Box 64383, Dept. K055-8
St. Paul, MN 55164-0383, U.S.A.
www.llewellyn.com

♻ Printed in the United States of America on recycled paper

Dedication

This book is dedicated to each reader who has been drawn to pick it up, read it, and hopefully be inspired to continue their own journey home. May your journey be made easier, quicker, and with a greater understanding and appreciation of the incredible potential within each one of us.

Acknowledgments

I'd like to recognize each person who has contributed to the material in this book. But since we all learn something from every single person that we meet, that would be a bit impractical. However, there are a few very special people who have guided me to where I am now, and I would like to publicly acknowledge their patience, kindness, wisdom, and special insights. They have gently pointed me toward a path that I had forgotten was so special and important to me: the path of healing. I am indeed indebted to my wonderful wife Anita for her untiring encouragement and support during the writing of this book. August Armstrong first awakened within me the faint stirrings of healing experiences from long ago, and Elaine Griffin introduced me to a very special group of loving and compassionate healers led by Dottie Graham, who opened my mind and heart to what we are capable of as spiritual human beings. And special thanks go to Patricia Hayes and Marshall Smith and the other wonderful teachers at Delphi University for providing the spiritual tools needed to prepare and develop myself as an instrument of healing for others. And lastly, thanks and gratitude go to all those spiritual beings who have lovingly chosen to guide my feet along this exciting new pathway home.

Namaste.

Contents

Chapter 1: Energy-Based Healing Concepts / 1

Chapter 2: Healing the Physical Energy Body / 45

Chapter 3: Healing the Etheric Energy Body / 69

Chapter 4: Healing the Emotional and Mental Energy Bodies / 79

Chapter 5: Awakening the Spiritual Energy Body / 121

Chapter 6: Growing Home / 131

Illustrations

Tables

Preface

It's good to be a seeker,
But sooner or later you have to be a finder.
And then it is well to give what you have found,
A gift into the world for whoever will accept it.

—Richard Bach, *Jonathan Livingston Seagull*

Each step we take along our own path in life awakens us to greater and grander vistas of who we are and why we are here doing the things we do. Each step we take in our realization as an individual allows us greater choices in the steps we lay before ourselves. My own childhood dream to become a doctor gave way to a career in engineering and scientific fields. Working for years as a well-established satellite communications systems engineer and technical program manager, one day I was led to a fork in the road that would change my career, my life, and how I perceived myself and others around me. One fork in the road read "Status Quo—Climb the Corporate Ladder," the other "Come Be A Healer and Learn About Yourself."

I chose the "Healing" fork. But I quickly found out that healing is not the end in the process; it is only the means to a greater end. As I use my tools of healing to help others and also to help myself, I begin to better understand the nature of my own reality. I do not recommend healing as the only or best way to gain greater insight into your own self, but it is the right way for me. Each person should find the way that resonates deep down inside them and says, "This is what I am really all about; this is what I am supposed to be doing."

When I was a young child, my family would drive several hours to the home of my grandparents in Seattle for festive holidays such as Thanksgiving and Christmas. One day I asked my grandmother about the picture of a mountain hanging in her kitchen. It was a great mountain that grew up out of a peaceful valley below to majestically high peaks covered with snow, and I wanted to know if it was nearby Mt. Rainier. "No," she said. "That is just a picture of life. There are a thousand pathways up the mountain, but they all lead to the same place. It does not really matter which path you choose, but *choose one* and *start walking!*"

As I grew up I began to understand her deep wisdom. We all come from different areas in the valley. Some look up and just wonder what the mountaintop would be like. Others have to start climbing from wherever they are to experience what is at the top, and to see the valley below from a higher perspective.

I had been working for a large company providing technical and engineering services in the satellite communications field to both the commercial and government sectors. I was leading a well-trained group of hardware and software engineers, and our company had just successfully negotiated an expanded contract for an additional five years. Everything was "coming up roses." Then one morning as I awoke, I heard a very clear and distinct voice say, "Howard, it's time!" I shot up in bed to see who was there, but the room was empty. At the same time, I knew completely what it was time for: it was time to move to the Virginia Beach, Virginia, area. But I did not know why at the time.

Several times during my life, I heard a very clear voice that would usually say something short like "No!" or "Don't do that!" or "Do not worry about this. It does not matter." Once while I was test-driving a car before I bought it, "The Voice" in my mind said very clearly and distinctly, "This car will be very reliable and economical to operate." I bought the car and have driven it more than 210,000 miles with no major repairs. Over the years I have learned to trust the advice given me by this unseen counselor. It has always been right, and always in my best interests. The one time I ignored The Voice and did not take its advice, I was placed in a situation that proved to be financially disastrous. Now, when The Voice speaks, I listen!

So when I heard "Howard, it's time!" I knew exactly what it was time for, and what I must do: move to Virginia Beach. That day I gave my notice at work and began preparations for moving, and within a few months, I had relocated to a comfortable house in the Chesapeake countryside with just over three acres. It was a welcome change from the pressure cooker of the Washington beltway scene. In just a few short weeks, doors began to open for me, and new opportunities to explore my own development suddenly presented themselves. First, I received a brochure in the mail for Reiki, a Japanese method of healing the physical body similar to laying-on-of-hands. Intrigued, I was soon initiated as a Reiki practitioner and began my fascinating odyssey with energy healing.

About the same time, I learned of workshops teaching other forms of physical healing such as Healing Touch, Reflexology, Shiatsu, Acupressure, and Polarity Therapy. Of these, I was particularly drawn to Healing Touch, and within several months had taken the first three workshops that taught all thirty individual Healing Touch techniques. While I was becoming familiar with the experience and practice of Healing Touch and Reiki, I attended a "get-away" weekend at Delphi University, a metaphysical institute in the Cherokee Hills of northern Georgia. There I was introduced to an eye-opening array of advanced healing techniques that included Ro-Hun, Reflective Healing, and Light Energization. Additional courses were also available for rapid development of one's natural intuitive abilities. I was hooked!

Over the next several years, my path was guided by my desire to help others in a down-to-earth practical way for physical and emotional healing, and a constant tug and pull on my inner psyche to heal and develop my own inner being. It has been said that you cannot heal others until you heal yourself. But I have also found that in learning how to bring healing to others, I have been able to bring healing to myself as well—not only physical healing, but also the comforting certainty and knowledge of what I am, who I am, and why I am here on this earth doing what I am doing. Knowing one's purpose in life, and being confident and comfortable in that purpose, is a strong motivator for fulfilling those inner urgings and yearnings we often tend to shove aside or ignore. I know that at least one of my purposes is to gather together the information and knowledge about our energetic nature from many diverse sources, and present it in this book for all who are ready to see, hear, and embrace the greater truth of what we are as humans, as well as our relationship to each other.

It is my hope that with this book I am able to inspire you to take a grand adventure up your own path on the mountainside of life. Let me point the way with illustrations from my own chosen path, healing. I hope this will provide an appreciation of the greater perspective of life and of ourselves as we keep climbing. I also hope that you will realize that a greater perspective and clearer purpose in life is really what we are all climbing toward, not just greater abilities as a healer, as a business person, as an artist, or whatever path you have chosen. That greater perspective and awareness of who we are as universal citizens is available to each mountain climber, not just those on the healing path. Come climb with me!

Introduction

In this high-tech age when we have split the atom, have walked on the moon, can talk to nearly anywhere in the world, and are inventing newer and better diagnostic machines to probe the human physiology, why are Americans returning in great numbers to a *simpler* form of medicine? Why have over two-thirds of the U.S. population tried one or more of the many forms of alternative treatments and healing techniques that are enjoying a recent and astounding revival?

Perhaps one reason is that we are steadily becoming aware that we are truly much more than just flesh and bones, tissue and organs, chemicals and minerals that all work together in an exquisite but delicate balance. As Eastern philosophies have taught for millennia, our multidimensional body also includes several invisible energy fields surrounding the physical body. These energy fields not only play a very large part in our physical health, they can also influence how we interact with our environment and others—emotionally, mentally, and spiritually.

However, until recently, training has not been available in our medical colleges for students, interns, and physicians to receive instruction and knowledge about the effect of these unseen human energy fields on the physical body. Instead, Western allopathic medicine has emphasized the use of drugs and surgery to treat disease. Modern surgical techniques and procedures are astounding in their ability to repair the human body, but often these techniques are not affordable or available to all who need them. Furthermore, the recent proliferation of new drugs has led to a situation where all physicians simply are not able to keep up with all the new drugs being produced. Side effects and unknown interactions between two or more drugs are also a real cause for concern.

In addition, most physicians no longer have time to discuss their patients' histories on anything but a clinical level. The time actually spent by the doctor discussing how the patient feels and why they might feel that way is shrinking more and more, and patients resent being quickly shuffled in and out of the doctor's office. Still, most physicians agree that how patients think and feel about themselves is a major factor in influencing their overall state of health.

Another significant factor in the changing landscape of medical treatment is that patients no longer simply accept what their doctor says at face value. They are more involved in their own health condition by becoming better informed on their own particular disease or symptoms, and are asking hard, detailed questions of their physicians regarding suggested treatment plans. They want information on disease *prevention,* not just disease treatment. Patients are beginning to take responsibility for their own health instead of leaving their health solely in the hands of their doctor. After all, it is their body!

And the more questions we ask, the more information we find about alternative, or nontraditional, methods of promoting health and healing the body of disease and symptoms. Books and magazine articles abound on the positive effects of diet, nutrition, acupuncture, herbs and vitamin supplements, homeopathic and naturopathic medicines, energy-based healing ("laying-on of hands"), chiropractic, meditation and prayer, and many other techniques to restore health to the complete emotional, mental, and spiritual human beings that we are.

So we need to become aware of emerging theories of health, disease, and treatment if we are to carry forward the best of traditional medical science, and at the same time incorporate alternative metaphysical healing techniques that have consistently proven effective. This will allow us to integrate these two approaches into the most effective, affordable, and complete healing regimen that eliminates disease and its symptoms on all levels. This is the new movement toward what is being called "Integrative Medicine."

In this book we will: (1) discuss basic principles and characteristics of the Human Energy Field surrounding each physical body, (2) present and describe several different types of energy-based healing techniques now becoming available for those seeking alternatives to traditional medical treatments, and (3) describe how they may be integrated into a truly holistic healing program addressing the physical, emotional, mental, and spiritual needs of the client.

If you are investigating alternative methods of healing, you have a steadily growing and often bewildering spectrum of techniques from which to choose. And the list seems to grow each time a new magazine article on the subject appears. But which healing techniques or modalities are recommended for addressing a specific disease or set of symptoms, and do they really work?

This book discusses several energy-based healing techniques that have repeatedly demonstrated a positive effect on clients who want to accelerate their healing process in a wide range of diseases. By "energy-based" healing techniques, I mean that subset of alternative healing techniques that makes use of the Human Energy Field, sometimes called the aura, of a trained healer to bring about a more harmonious energy field in the client. This can result in greater overall physical health in the client, as well as a more balanced and healthy aura.

But I want the reader to be skeptical of what is presented here—keep an *open* mind, but do not let your brain fall out! Do not just automatically believe what you read. You need to decide if it makes sense to you. Does it fit into the information and belief systems you use in your daily life, or is it too "radical" for you to consider at this time? A wise man once said, "Don't *believe* anything for more than two hours." If you can not see and feel the truth of it within that time, just put it up on the shelf until it makes sense to include it as part of your own evolving truth. But do not prejudge anything just because you do not understand it. As we continue to experience new situations and learn from them, our own personal truth expands to include this new knowledge.

For now, you the reader will have to *believe* or *not believe* in the truth of what you read here. But if you experience a healing as either the healer or the client, then you will come to know the truth of it for yourself, either positive or negative. You will not have to believe with blind faith what is written here. If you know for a fact that your healing experience is real, you can then freely take the knowledge of that experience into your own truth, and your awareness will expand to include a new realization of what we are all capable of.

This book also addresses several questions regarding the current state of energy healing. What kinds of alternative healing techniques are available? Can energy-based healing techniques be used to cure disease? Is healing temporary, or can energy-based healing provide a *permanent* cure? What does a "healer" really do? Is healing a special gift for only a few, or can anyone learn to be a healer? How can energy-based healing techniques and traditional medical treatment be integrated into an overall holistic program to provide a permanent cure for a specific disease? These and other intriguing questions are discussed in detail in the hopes that this additional information can help provide a personal road map for greater health that meets the specific needs of each seeker.

What kinds of alternative healing techniques are available? Chiropractic, acupuncture, massage therapy, natural remedies, flower essences, vibrational sound therapy, homeopathic medicine, Ayurvedic medicine, and energy-based techniques such as Reiki, Healing Touch, Polarity, Johrei, Bioenergy, etc., are only a small fraction of those available. Many insurance companies are now beginning to cover many of these alternative techniques simply because people get well more quickly, require less medication, have fewer complications, and stay less time in hospitals when a balanced program of traditional and alternative medical therapies are used.

Of the many different categories of alternative therapies now available (such as natural herbs and remedies, structural integration techniques, yoga and meditation exercises, energy-based techniques, etc.), this book concentrates on several specific *energy-based* techniques. These techniques have been repeatedly shown to be effective and can be easily integrated into an overall holistic healing program tailored for a specific individual. These techniques address healing of not only the physical body, but also of the higher energy bodies in the Human Energy Field.

Can energy-based healing techniques be used to cure disease? Yes, but here we must understand the difference between treatment and healing. Many traditional medical procedures involve the treatment of disease symptoms, such as the pain associated with arthritis or a life-threatening cancerous growth, through drugs or surgery. Although these techniques can be very effective in the short term, they merely mask or control the symptoms of the disease instead of removing the original cause of the disease. For example, a cancerous organ may be simply removed from the body rather than eliminating the *cause* of the cancer. However, both drugs and surgery are powerful tools that can provide improved conditions for the body to heal itself. Yet in many cases, the disease may recur for reasons that may not be completely understood. We will examine in depth the reasons disease occasionally recurs.

But can energy-based healing provide a permanent cure? When we remove the cause of a disease as well as its symptoms, we have gone beyond just treating the disease; we have ensured that the reason the disease exists is completely removed, and we can be confident that it will not recur. This is true healing, and is accomplished through a holistic healing program that is much more comprehensive than only the traditional medical techniques in use today. If a holistic approach is adopted that addresses all levels of a person's being (physical, emotional, mental, and spiritual), the healing is usually permanent. The range of energy-based healing techniques discussed here provides a holistic approach to healing all levels of a person's being; these techniques can also be supplemented by additional lifestyle changes such as diet, exercise, and stress reduction.

What does a "healer" really do? An energy-based healer has been trained to channel or direct healing energies into a client for the purpose of healing. Energy-based healers have also been trained to see, sense, or feel the various layers of the client's energy field, or aura. And, depending on the specific healing technique involved, the healer has been trained in specific procedures to alter or "repattern" the client's energy field in a positive way such that the result is greater health.

Is healing a special gift, or can anyone learn to be a healer? Often the answer is both. Some people are born with a special ability to heal, and some are given this gift later in life. Still other healers have developed the innate healing ability that is in each of us to varying degrees. One example is Mietek Wirkus, a Polish healer who, at the age of six, was repeatedly able to stop his sister's asthma attacks merely by placing his hand on her arm. He later developed his own healing technique called "Bioenergy," which he teaches to others. Another example is "Mr. A" whose story is told in Ruth Montgomery's bestseller *Born to Heal.*[1] Examples of people who were given special healing gifts later in life are Buddha and Jesus. On the other hand, I am an example of one who has developed my own innate healing abilities through instruction, self-development, and continuing experience in my own healing practice.

What should the client expect by going to an energy healer? This depends both on the healing technique received (Reiki, Reflective Healing, etc.), and the individual healer's style and preferences. If you came to me for any of the techniques discussed in this book, you would be asked to remove only your shoes, jewelry, and any crystals, and lie down on a comfortably padded healing table. I usually have soft, relaxing music playing in the background. Pillows are provided for your comfort, and a blanket if you wish. During some techniques such as Reiki or Healing Touch, you may choose to stay very alert or drop into a state of relaxation for the duration of the healing session. During other techniques such as Hypnotherapy or Ro-Hun, you may be placed into a deeply relaxed state, but will remain conscious of everything that goes on so you can conduct an active dialogue with the therapist during the session. Other specific details and procedures are discussed in the chapters for each healing technique.

How can energy-based healing techniques and traditional medical treatment be integrated into an overall holistic program to provide a permanent cure for a specific disease? The most important ingredient in a holistic healing program are knowledgeable clients who are well informed about both traditional medical procedures as they apply to their own specific disease/symptoms, and also about the available alternative therapies which may be of benefit to their health.

More and more, individuals are becoming responsible and proactive for their own health programs and treatment regimens. They are educating themselves in the medical options available to them. They are discussing the details of their proposed treatment program with their doctors. And they are also becoming aware of the alternative medical therapies that are available, and are asking their doctors how these therapies may be used to complement the doctor's traditional medical knowledge and surgical skills.

It is heartening to note that nearly all of the medical universities in the United States now offer courses in alternative medical therapies, although it is usually as an elective. Nevertheless, doctors are becoming aware of a wider range of therapies that can be used against specific diseases and conditions. They, like their patients, are beginning to understand the complex and intricate mechanism of the human body and the interaction of its energy field with others' fields. Both the doctor/healer and patient/client are becoming more aware of their roles. Overall physical health can be improved and disease eliminated by using techniques that address the entire being on the physical, emotional, mental, and spiritual levels of each person.

To understand energy-based healing and the principles that allow one to be a conduit or channel of healing energy for another, we must begin by understanding the energetic nature of our bodies. Chapter 1 provides the reader with a discussion of the Universal Energy Field and the Human Energy Field, along with an overview of energetic principles as they relate to human healing, and as I understand them at this point in my own development. Chapters 2 through 5 provide a discussion of those significant modalities which pertain to the healing on the physical level (Healing Touch and Reiki), etheric level (Spiritual

Surgery and Reflective Healing), emotional and mental levels (Ro-Hun and Hypnotherapy), and the spiritual level (Light Energization). Lastly, chapter 6 provides a summation and overview from a broader perspective of the principles and information in the first five chapters.

It should be noted here that the modalities chosen for discussion are only a small fraction of the available energy-based healing techniques, and this is not to imply that the ones examined are the best or most effective modalities. I have elected to discuss these because they are the ones to which I have been guided and drawn, and because I have received detailed training and practical experience with each of them. They are all included in my own healing practice.

Energy-Based
Healing Concepts

The human energy field responds to stimuli even before the brain does. I think we have way overrated the brain as the active ingredient in the relationship of a human to the world. The mind's not in the brain. It's in that darn field.

—Valerie Hunt, quoted by Michael Talbot
in *The Holographic Universe*

Since the beginning of time, humans have looked up at the nighttime sky and wondered how many stars exist, and how far away they are. Intricate designs of animals, warriors, and other symbols were seen in the heavens, and these patterns and constellations were used to interpret the cycles of life on this great planet. Then, as telescopes and other instruments were used and these stars were closely observed, the then-prevalent geocentric concept of the universe began to crumble, and a new awareness emerged of our place in the universe—the earth was no longer the center of the universe. It was now but merely one of several planets which circle our sun, which is in turn just one of the infinite number of stars in the heavens.

As instruments improved and several scientific branches of investigation examined the heavens, we began to estimate the size, shape, and mass of the universe. However, as astronomers gaze deeper into the heavens, they continue to come across processes in other galaxies and other worlds for which they have no explanation. Clearly, our present understanding of the composition of the universe is less than perfect.

In an attempt to correct this situation, astronomers and astrophysicists have begun to reexamine some of their basic theories and concepts of nature. The Newtonian concept of our physical world worked very well when we were not aware of the vast fields of energy that permeate all levels of the universe, from the largest galaxies to the smallest atom. Not only is Newtonian physics being reevaluated, but also the limitations of Einstein's Theory of Relativity are now apparent. However, Einstein's famous equation $E=mc^2$ stated a fundamental truth that energy and matter are interchangeable. We have learned how to transform matter into energy through the atomic fission process. In addition, we have now demonstrated in the laboratory a limited capability to create matter using only focused beams of light from high-energy lasers.

The Universal Energy Field

There appears to be a source of energy within our universe that is, as yet, unexplained. However, more than one physicist has speculated that our universe began its existence as a subtle energy field of very high vibrational frequencies, and in some places this field gradually became denser and denser over time, with subsequently lower vibrational patterns. Eventually, these areas of denser vibrational patterns coalesced into what we now perceive as our physical universe of galaxies, stars, and planets. It is also speculated that, in the immensity of space within our universe, the energy field from which all matter coalesced is still there. This original energy field is of a higher vibratory rate and is theorized to contain the holographic pattern for all physical creation. This vast sea of vibrational energy is beyond the reach of today's instruments, and is termed the Universal Energy Field, or UEF.

In her groundbreaking book on energy-based healing, *Hands of Light*, Barbara Brennan lists several potential characteristics of the UEF. According to Brennan, the UEF is probably composed of a type of energy previously undefined by Western science, and which may exist in a state between what we consider matter and energy. Furthermore she speculates that this energy permeates all animate and inanimate objects in the universe, and connects all objects with each other. It can also be perceived or sensed by our inner senses of touch, taste, smell, sound, and luminosity (not the five normal physical senses). Lastly, she suggests that this energy consistently is creative in that it is consistently building form, as opposed to degenerating form; that is, it is synergistic instead of entropic.[1]

If Brennan's observations are accurate, we are indeed becoming aware of our universe as much, much more than we can see and measure with today's instruments.

The Human Energy Field

The Human Energy Field (HEF) is "that part of the UEF associated with the human body."[2] The HEF can be described in three different ways: in terms of (1) the major and minor chakras throughout the body, (2) the subtle energy fields or energy bodies that surround the physical body, and (3) the energy meridians within the physical body that provide the means of circulating and distributing energy (also called prana, chi, or ki) to the tissues and organs of the body. Each of these perspectives is discussed below.

The Chakra System

The Sanskrit word "chakra" means literally "spinning wheel." To those who can see energy fields, a major chakra resembles a spinning wheel when looking directly into the chakra. However, viewed from the side, it looks more like an energy vortex somewhat resembling the shape of a tornado. This energy funnel is tight and compact near the surface of the skin, and gradually widens as it extends outside the physical body to the edge of the aura.

The chakra system within the human body consists of seven major chakras and many minor chakras. The location of the seven major chakras is shown in Figure 1 (see page 4). Each major chakra from the Root through the Brow has four energy vortices associated with it: one spiraling upward, one downward toward the earth, one out the front of the body, and one out through the back of the body. The upward projecting vortex from one chakra and the downward projecting vortex of

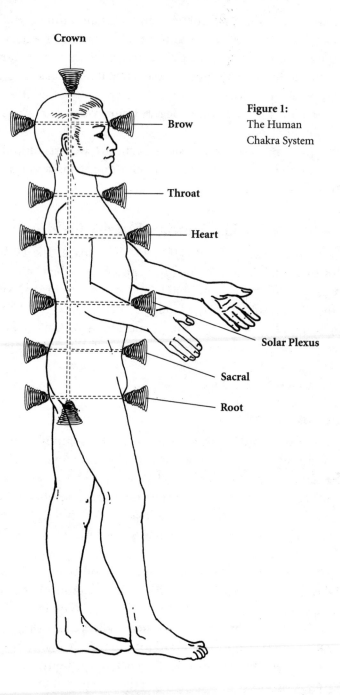

Crown

Brow

Throat

Heart

Solar Plexus

Sacral

Root

Figure 1:
The Human
Chakra System

the chakra just above it, join to form an energy column that runs vertically through the physical body from the bottom of the spine (Root Chakra) up in front of the spine and out through the top of the head (Crown Chakra). The Crown Chakra has two vortices, one opening upward toward the heavens, and one projecting downward into the energy column running through the body.

When a chakra is "healthy and balanced" its front and rear vortices spin in a circular motion. However, if there is a disturbance or blockage in the flow of energy within a chakra, the circular motion may become elliptical or, in extreme cases, severely flattened on its sides. This distortion may be sensed by those able to see or feel energy fields, or indirectly sensed by a pendulum (to be discussed later). Furthermore, each chakra has its own specific "frequency," or rate of spin, with the lowest rate of spin in the Root Chakra, and steadily increasing up to the highest rate of spin in the Crown Chakra.

The purpose or function of the human chakra system is to take in higher-dimensional energy from the Universal Energy Field all around us and translate or "step down" its frequency of vibration to that which can be used within the physical body. Each major chakra vibrates or spins at a different rate, and each chakra will absorb energy from the UEF that is harmonically related to its own frequency. Thus, energy from several frequency bands within the UEF is absorbed by the different chakras and is directed to those organs with which that chakra is associated (see Table A, page 6). A good analogy of how this occurs is to visualize all the many TV signals existing around us all the time; by tuning to a specific channel (frequency), we get the specific information or programming being sent on that frequency. The human chakra system can then be said to act as a sort of "multichannel receiver" of vibrations from different portions of the energy spectrum all around us.

Through the internal human energy distribution system (see "Energy Meridians" on page 13), each chakra is connected to specific organs and endocrine glands, as shown in the previous table. For instance, the particular energy vibrations or frequencies absorbed by the Solar Plexus Chakra are linked energetically to the stomach, pancreas, gall bladder, and liver. Likewise, the reproductive organs receive

Chakra	Associated Organs	Endocrine Gland
Crown	Upper Brain, Right Eye	Pineal
Brow	Ears, Nose, Lower Brain, Nervous System, Left Eye	Pituitary
Throat	Lungs, Larnyx, Alimentary Canal	Thyroid, Parathyroid
Heart	Heart, Blood, Vagus Nerve, Circulatory System	Thymus
Solar Plexus	Stomach, Gallbladder, Liver	Pancreas
Sacral	Reproductive System	Testes, Ovaries
Root	Spinal Column, Kidneys	Adrenals

Table A: Major Chakras and Associated Organs and Glands

their components of energy from the UEF through the Sacral Chakra (sometimes called the Spleen or Splenic Chakra).[3]

Many minor chakras are also located throughout the body, and are usually associated with joints such as the knee, shoulder, elbow, etc. Additional minor chakras are found in the palms of both hands, the soles of the feet, and the ends of the fingers and toes. These minor chakras appear as spikes of energy emanating from the body rather than the spinning vortices of the major chakras. As will be discussed later, at least one major healing modality (Healing Touch) takes advantage of these rays of energy coming out of the fingertips to stimulate and accelerate the body's own healing processes.

Energy Body	Contents, Characteristics
Physical	The physical body, organs, cells, and tissues with which we are familiar.
Etheric	An etheric matrix of energy gridlines upon which the cells of our bodies grow and take form. The "blueprint" for the physical body. Whatever pattern is present in the Etheric Body will, in time, be reflected in the Physical Body.
Emotional	The feelings and emotional patterns which are formed in response to the beliefs and thoughts in the Mental Body. Sometimes called the Astral Body.
Mental	The cultural and personal belief systems and thoughts about one's self and how one interacts with others.
Spiritual	Your higher purposes, goals, intentions, and inner senses for accomplishing the greatest good possible. Your "conscience," and your sense of connection with others, your environment, the universe, and your Source.

Table B: Energy Bodies of the Human Energy Field

Energy Bodies

The Human Energy Field, or aura, is made up of a number of individual but harmonically related energetic bodies, each vibrating at its own frequency. All these subtle energy bodies are actually spatially superimposed over the physical form. Above the vibrational energy of the physical body are the Etheric Body, the Emotional Body, the Mental Body, and the Spiritual Body.[4] This is not to say that finer gradations do not exist; however, the groupings chosen are adequate to discuss the healing modalities presented here. Each energy body surrounds and interpenetrates all lower energy bodies, including the physical body. For example, the Emotional Body surrounds and penetrates the Etheric and Physical Bodies. The human energy bodies are depicted in Figure 2 (see page 9) and are described in Table B (see above).

If it is difficult to visualize the superimposed and interpenetrating energy bodies of our Human Energy Field, then think of the many radio and TV signals that are penetrating your body and existing simultaneously within the same space as your body. Moving through all "solid" matter is a constant barrage of vibrations that is far above our ability to detect with our physical senses. Tune into the right frequency with the proper receiver, and you can listen to your favorite radio station; tune in to even higher frequencies and you get the evening news on Channel 12. Above these frequencies are heat, light, ultraviolet radiation, x-rays, and highly energetic particles of cosmic radiation. All these vibrations exist simultaneously within the same three-dimensional space that our body occupies, and the only characteristic that differentiates one from another is frequency, the rate at which that particular "kind" of energy vibrates.

The Physical Energy Body   At first, it may seem unusual to consider that the physical body is an energy body, but that is exactly what it appears to be. And as we explore and become more accustomed to this new paradigm, we are able not only to see the physical body in a greater, more meaningful context, but also we begin to understand the role of disease and the nature of healing. The physical body is the densest form of energy that our consciousness uses to explore its environment and interact with others. By the densest form, I mean that the vibrational patterns of the physical body are of a frequency low enough to be seen by our eyes (they are within the spectrum of visible light), heard by our ears (about 30 to 15,000 Hertz), and experienced with the senses of touch, taste, and smell within the "frequency capability" of our physical body.

But there are many octaves, frequencies, and vibrations beyond the capability of our physical senses. Beyond what we can see as visible light are the higher frequencies of ultraviolet, x-ray, and cosmic radiation. We are beginning to understand that what we can physically sense is only a small portion of the vibrational energies around us. If we look within our physical bodies at our atoms, molecules, and cells, again we find patterns of vibrating energy that we have traditionally called "matter."

We need to become aware that our physical body is really a field of vibrating energy that has coalesced from higher, less dense octaves. But we

Figure 2:
Energy Bodies
of the Human
Energy System

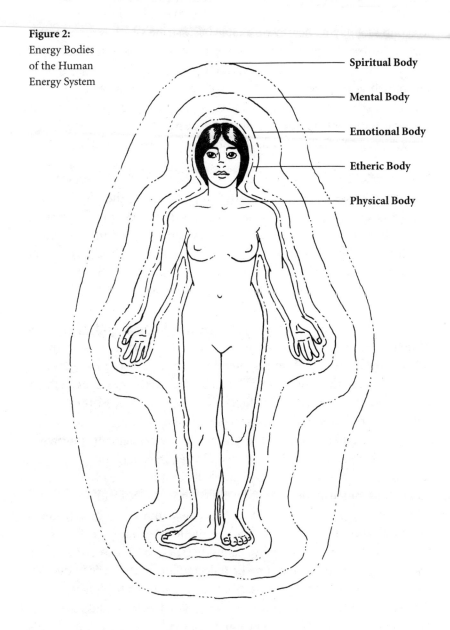

Spiritual Body

Mental Body

Emotional Body

Etheric Body

Physical Body

also need to remember that as vibrating fields interact with each other, one field can affect another field through the phenomenon of sympathetic vibration. If a violin player produces a note an octave above Middle C, and a second violin lying nearby on a table has a string which is tuned to Middle C, the second violin string tuned to Middle C will sympathetically begin to vibrate as well. So as we also begin to understand that there are several vibrational fields of energy around our physical body, it becomes easier to understand how one field affects another through this principle. And this is the key to understanding how energy-based healing techniques can achieve such visible and profound results in the physical body.

The Etheric Energy Body The etheric body is the first energy body in frequency above the physical body. It exists within the physical body, and extends outward about an inch outside the skin of the physical body. Its purpose is to form an energy template, or matrix, for the development, maintenance, and repair of the physical body. The etheric body contains a vibrational energy counterpart for each organ, blood vessel, and bone found in the physical body. Indeed, the etheric body contains the energetic blueprint for the pathways that guide the location and development of every cell of the physical body. "The bony structure, muscular, and vascular tissues, the nerves, the brain, and other substances are all represented in the etheric mold by currents of energy on specific frequencies."[5] "The physical tissues exist as such only because of the vital (etheric) field behind them; that is, the (etheric) field is prior to, not a result of, the physical body."[6]

Since the etheric body is the physical body's blueprint, the two are very closely related. As will be discussed later, the energetic vibrations of the etheric body determine the pattern for not only the physical tissues and organs, but also the state of health of those tissues and organs. If the vibrations are not clear and pure, this disharmony will be reflected in the physical body as disharmonious function—what we call "disease." Conversely, traumas to the physical body (such as broken bones, burns, incisions, and scars) will in time be reflected into the etheric body unless there is some interceding process that either prevents this reflection into the etheric body or which restores the original vibrational pattern that existed prior to the trauma. The ability to work with a client's vibrating energy fields is precisely what forms the basis for rapid and effective energy-based physical healings.

As explained by Talbot, an illness can appear in the energy field weeks and even months before it appears in the physical body. He considers that the physical body "is just one more level of density in the human energy field and is itself a kind of hologram that has coalesced out of the interference patterns of the aura . . ."[7] Richard Gerber, a Detroit physician, agrees, noting that "the etheric body is a holographic energy template that guides the growth and development of the physical body."[8]

The following description of the etheric and higher subtle energy bodies surrounding the physical body are taken from Brennan's book, *Hands of Light*. To those who can directly observe energy fields, the etheric body appears as a grid of tiny energy lines with the overall structure and shape of the physical body. This matrix extends from a quarter-inch to two inches beyond the physical body. It is upon this etheric grid or matrix that the cells and tissues of the body develop and are anchored. The etheric body appears as a light blue or gray matrix of lines of light that constantly pulsate or scintillate at a rate of from 15–20 cycles per minute.[9]

The Emotional Energy Body The emotional body contains the emotional patterns, feelings, and vibrations that determine our personality, and also how we feel about ourselves and interact with others. If we are constantly angry, always feel helpless, or are consistently fearful, these patterns or vibrations get locked in our emotional energy field and become a part of our personality. This determines to a very large degree how we interact with others on personal, social, and cultural levels.

The emotional body generally follows the shape of the physical and etheric bodies, but is somewhat more amorphous and fluid, and extends from one to about three inches outside the physical body. It contains energy "blobs" of all colors of the rainbow, depending on the specific feeling or emotion. Highly charged feelings such as love, hate, joy, and anger are associated with energy blobs that are bright and clear, while confused feelings are darker and muddier.

The Mental Energy Body The mental body contains the structure and patterns of all the thoughts and belief systems that we consider as true. There is a very strong connection between the mental and emotional bodies. Although a thought or idea can in itself be very powerful, our reactions to those thoughts carry even more energy, and different people will react differently to the same thought. For example, consider the thought form "If you are not a Catholic (or Protestant, or Muslim, or Jew, or whatever), you cannot go to Heaven." One person might hear that thought or idea, think it was silly, and give it absolutely no energy. But another person might become very passionate, depending on his greater belief systems, and argue strongly either for or against the truth of that statement. His emotional body would then record the intensity of the reaction to the thought stored in the mental body. However, the person who thought the statement was silly in the first place would not have any resonance with it, and no energetic pattern would be stored in either the mental or emotional bodies.

The mental body usually appears as yellow light radiating around the entire body from head to toe, and extends from three to eight inches beyond the physical body. Within this area, individual thought forms appear as small blobs of light of varying form and intensity.

The Spiritual Energy Body The spiritual body (that is, all vibrational patterns in octaves higher than the mental body) contains all the information related to our experiences, and reflects our gestalt consciousness of all that has been learned and experienced. It contains our higher intentions, our sense of what is right and wrong ("conscience"), and our desires to increase our awareness of our purpose, place, and mission for this lifetime.

These five energy bodies make up a person's Human Energy Field, or aura. Its outer shape appears roughly egg-shaped and extends out to approximately one and one-half to two feet beyond the physical body; however, this shape can be extended even further out or contracted closer to the physical body depending on the situation the person is experiencing. For example, when a person feels emotions of unconditional love, the aura may expand to several feet and radiate bright hues of gold or white; but if the same person is feeling threatened physically or emotionally, the entire aura may collapse to a much denser pattern within only a few inches of the body.

Chapters 2 through 5 provide examples of different energy-based techniques that provide healing on these physical, etheric, emotional/mental and spiritual levels, respectively.

Energy Meridians

Within the body many energetic pathways connect each organ and chakra, both major and minor. It is this internal energy distribution system which permits the flow of life-sustaining energy to the internal organs and tissues. This system of pathways has been known and used for several thousand years by Oriental practitioners of acupuncture. In acupuncture, or acupressure, the thought is that many diseases are caused or exacerbated by inadequate energy flow to certain areas of the body or organs. The fine needles used in acupuncture stimulate specific points on these energy meridians to release the blocked flow of life-force energy, and thus restore health. More recently, acupressure, a variation of this practice, has become quite popular. With acupressure, stimulation of the energy meridians to release the blocked flow of energy is accomplished through pressure from the fingers or hands instead of acupuncture needles. Western medicine is just now beginning to recognize the effectiveness of acupuncture and acupressure and, encouragingly, some insurance companies are now allowing payments for acupuncture and acupressure simply because patients recover quicker, and with fewer complications.

The chapters that follow describe several healing modalities for modulating the energy components of the physical and subtle energy bodies of the client. However, for the modalities discussed, it is not necessary to have a detailed understanding of the energy meridian system within the physical body. It is enough to recognize that when healing energy is transferred to the client's body through whatever means (such as the healer placing his hands on the client in a Reiki session), the energy meridians within the body provide a means of distributing the energy from the healer to wherever it is needed within the body.

The Nature of Healing Energy

A number of very interesting studies and carefully controlled experiments have been conducted to determine the nature of the healing energies exhibited by healers' hands. These studies have provided strong evidence to suggest that healing energy is magnetic in nature, as opposed to the electrical energy exhibited by the physical body. We are all familiar with the electroencephalograph (EEG), which measures the minute electrical currents within the brain, and the electrocardiogram (EKG), which measures the minute electrical currents within the heart and other body tissues. But only since the development of the ultrasensitive magnetic field detector called a SQUID (Super-conducting QUantum Interference Device) has it been possible to measure and document the intensity of the magnetic field emitted by a healer's hands.

In his book *Vibrational Medicine,* Dr. Richard Gerber cites the interesting work of Dr. John Zimmerman and several others, and states that Zimmerman, working at the University of Colorado School of Medicine, found that during a healing session the intensity of the magnetic field of the healer's hands increased to several hundred times that of the background noise.[10] Research chemist Robert Miller found copper sulphate solution exposed to either strong magnetic fields or the magnetic field of a healer's hands will always form coarse-grained turquoise-blue crystals, instead of the usual jade-green structures formed in the absence of a magnetic field.

Dr. Justa Smith found that "healers can accelerate the kinetic activity of enzymes in a fashion similar to the effects of high-intensity magnetic fields."[11] Using several different enzymes, she also found one (NAD-ase) which exhibited increased activity when exposed to a strong magnetic field, but showed a reduction in activity when exposed to a healer's hands. However, when the cellular metabolic functions of this enzyme were examined, it turned out that a decrease in enzyme activity caused, or was strongly correlated with, a greater energy reserve within the cell. In another experiment, Dr. Smith purposely damaged the enzyme trypsin by exposing it to a strong ultraviolet light. The damaged enzyme was then held in the hands of a healer, and the structural integrity and organization of the enzyme was restored.

Therefore, Gerber has concluded: "The activity of the enzymes affected by the healers always seemed to be in a direction that was toward greater overall health and balanced metabolic activity of the organism. . . . The suggestion here is that the subtle life-energies of healers seem to have primarily magnetic properties."[12] Gerber also points out that, through the instrument of their hands, the healer transfers these magnetic-like energies primarily to the physical body and its closely connected energetic template, the etheric body. A very strong and plausible case is made for the argument that while the matter of the physical body is primarily electrical in nature, the matter of the etheric body is primarily magnetic in nature. It is recommended that the serious investigator consider Gerber's documentation and theories.

Sensing Energy Fields

In order to promote healing, the energy-based healing practitioner must modulate or manipulate one or more of the various energy bodies, including the physical body. This is normally done through a combination of hand motions and the healer's intentions. However, in order to manipulate an energy body, the healer must somehow be able to accurately locate it; if the healer intended to manipulate the etheric body, that result could not be achieved if the practitioner's hands were held higher only in the client's mental field.

There are several methods of sensing where each subtle energy body is located, as well as sensing the vibrational activity of the chakras. Some healers are clairvoyantly sensitive to energy and can actually see the vibrational movement within each separate energy body. However, this is not very common. Most energy practitioners can physically sense the presence of energy fields and spinning chakra energy vortices with their hands or fingers; this is a skill that can be easily learned by nearly anyone. And finally, a simple pendulum can be used to dowse the vibrational condition of energy centers such as the chakras. Each of these methods is discussed below.

Directly Viewing Energy Fields

Some people are able to visually or intuitively see the energy field of others. One such person is Barbara Brennan, author of *Hands of Light*. In this book she has provided several color illustrations of how each subtle energy body appears to her. In addition, several examples of energy disturbances that result in disease or symptoms are shown. For the vast majority of healers who have not yet developed what she calls their "Higher Sense Perception," and the ability to see energy, these illustrations are indeed most impressive. Yet she is also the first to say that the illustrations show only how energy appears to her, and that it may appear differently to another person.

Dowsing with a Pendulum

A pendulum is a small object suspended (or "pendled") on a thread or string about six to eight inches long, and is used primarily to determine the state of the spinning vibrational energy of a chakra. As the pendulum is moved into the vortex of the chakra, it begins to move in response to the chakra energy. The direction of movement of the pendulum can be observed, and the energetic state of the chakra can be inferred from this movement. The pendulum is responding to the interaction of the healer's energetic field (aura), and the field of the client being dowsed or pendled.

The pendulum is also very useful for visually observing the condition of the energy in a minor chakra such as a joint. For example, in one of the Healing Touch techniques, each vertebral joint of the spine can be tested with a pendulum to determine if there is a smooth energy flow through the joint. Alternatively, there may be an energy blockage found contributing to the physical back symptoms experienced by the client.

The pendulum can make several different types of movement, and each can be related to a specific energetic condition of the chakra being monitored. Normally, a rotation of the pendulum in a circle of about an inch or two in diameter indicates a "healthy" energy condition within the chakra, whereas movement of the pendulum in a straight line might indicate that an energy block exists in the chakra pendled. In between the circular and straight movements is an elliptical motion which might indicate that the chakra energy is still flowing, but in a reduced or distorted manner.

When dowsing or pendling the major chakras, it is also important to pay attention to the size of the circle, ellipse, or line that is traced by the pendulum. In a healthy aura, all major chakras will cause the pendulum to move in about the same size diameter. Therefore, you should not be alarmed if you see a circle of only one inch in diameter for all chakras.

But if the pendulum spins in a two-inch diameter circle over all chakras except one spinning with only a one-inch diameter, you could correctly infer that some physical or energetic condition is inhibiting that chakra's full functioning.

Each practitioner who uses a pendulum usually has a favorite material for the pendulum. Many prefer quartz crystals, some prefer certain types of wood, and others use a favorite ornament on their "special" necklace. However, the weight of the pendulum may have more to do with its response than the type of material it is made of. I have made and successfully used pendulums of conducting metal, insulators such as plastic or glass, a paper clip, wood of all types, stone beads, brass nuts, and a chip of ceramic tile. They all worked equally well, with the main difference being that the heavier pendulums took longer to start rotating, and usually had a smaller diameter circle than the lighter pendulums. Also, the length and weight of the string or line connected to the pendulum will have an effect. The longer the length, the slower the pendulum will rotate and (eventually) the wider the circle will be. There is no way to say what should be the right length, weight, and material for you. Start with a string length of six to eight inches, and try several materials that "feel" good to you, and give you a reliable response from client to client.

In order to receive consistent results from a pendulum, it must be programmed to respond to a specific set of conditions in the body in a certain way. For instance, you can specify that the pendulum's reaction to a "normal" healthy chakra be a circular motion, and a blocked chakra be observed by a horizontal back-and-forth movement across the chakra. You could just as easily program the pendulum to respond in the reverse manner. The essential component that determines how your pendulum will respond is your intention!

A good example of this power of intention can be demonstrated by programming your pendulum to respond to "Yes" or "Positive" in one direction (e.g., toward and away from your body if you are holding the pendulum in front of you) and "No" or "Negative" in a perpendicular direction (e.g., sideways across your body). To program it in this manner, simply concentrate your vision and mental focus on the pendulum, and say aloud or to yourself, "I intend that a motion of this pendulum toward and away from my body represents 'Yes' or 'Positive,' and a motion across my body represents 'No' or 'Negative.'" It is that simple.

To test the pendulum, hold your left hand horizontally in front of you with your palm down and your fingers spread far apart. Now, holding the pendulum string in your right hand, place the body of the pendulum about an inch in front of the tip of your left index finger. In a moment, it will start to move in the direction that you have programmed for Positive or Yes (either parallel or perpendicular to your finger). Now move the pendulum to about an inch from the tip of your middle finger, and it will begin to move in the direction that you have programmed for Negative. This corresponds to the positive and negative polarities of the energy meridians that extend through your fingers. This "spike" of energy extends several inches beyond the end of your fingertips.

Now for the fun part. Reprogram your pendulum in just the reverse fashion to respond to a "Positive" or "Yes" with a horizontal motion back and forth across your body, and a "Negative" or "No" with a horizontal motion toward and away from your body, and retest the same index and middle fingers. Miraculously, you will observe the newly programmed motion in the pendulum! Truly this is mind over matter, and there is no way to misinterpret what you have just seen. The intention you stated in the thought form (programming your pendulum) has caused the pendulum to move in a certain direction, and by changing your thought form, you are able to change how you influence a material object!

The movement of the pendulum can also be used by the energy practitioner to determine the state of a particular chakra on each energy level. A chakra that moves in a circular motion in the etheric body, for example, may have a completely different motion (e.g., elliptical or straight) in the emotional body. Through intention and the ability to sense the separate energy bodies, the practitioner can ask the pendulum to indicate, for example, the state of the Solar Plexus Chakra on the mental level or on the emotional level. This allows complete characterization of the state of the chakra on all levels within the aura.

Still another fascinating property of the pendulum is its ability to respond to Yes/No questions according to the way you have programmed it. When held in front of you where you can see it clearly, ask a question aloud which can be unambiguously answered by Yes or No, and the pendulum will respond. However, in this case the pendulum is responding to the energetic response made by your Higher Self, your soul, or your spirit. Once you become familiar with the operation of the pendulum, you can easily use it in this way to provide infallible guidance that will always be in your best interests.

Scanning with Your Hand

While the pendulum may be used to get an approximate quantitative evaluation of the state of a chakra, your own hand can provide additional qualitative information about the client's energy bodies. Once the energy healer's hands are developed to sense or feel energy, the healer can use them to directly determine the overall shape of the outer edge of the aura, the boundaries of the inner energy bodies (e.g., etheric/emotional or emotional/mental boundaries), the shape of a chakra within each energy body out to the edge of the aura, and the location and qualities of any areas of energy abnormalities within the energy bodies.

How energy feels, however, is unique to each individual, and each person may have a different sensation when scanning or running his hand through the energy field of the same client. For example, an area of energy congestion may feel scratchy, hot, "angry or prickly" to one healer, and another healer may have a sense of vibration in his hands or fingers at the same location. The sensations that are felt by the healer are the result of the interaction of his field with that of the client, and it may be a very different reaction with a different client. Therefore, it is important not to anticipate what you think the sensation might be, but instead to recognize how the energy feels when you first sense it, and to detect changes in the way it feels as the session progresses.

To scan a client's energy field with my hand, I usually start by getting an impression of the overall shape of the aura at its outer edge. Starting from several feet away from the client, I move my hands in slowly over one area of the client's body (such as the abdomen) until I sense the outer edge of the spiritual energy body in that area. Then I repeat this in enough locations to get a rough idea of the overall shape of the aura. Particular attention is paid to the regions of the aura directly over the front chakras, Root through Brow. Normally, the aura will be symmetrical around the client. If there is any deviation noted from this symmetry, it is very useful to document it. This will allow comparison with later scans following the energy sessions.

After the shape of the aura is determined, the individual chakra vortices may be scanned with the hand to gain any additional information beyond that obtained from the pendulum. If abnormalities are noticed in the etheric layer of a chakra, this may give the healer a clue as to which organs may be affected and what symptoms might be presented. Similarly, when the emotional and mental bodies are scanned by a sensitive healer, different sensations such as hot, cold, scratchy, jagged, or a strong vibration may indicate the presence of a block in the natural flow of energy on these levels. This could, in turn, indicate the source of symptoms that appear in the physical.

For example, a mental belief that you are unworthy of success (mental layer) may result in a feeling of anger at yourself (emotional layer). In accordance with the principle of resonance through sympathetic vibrations, this in turn affects the etheric layer, which is the blueprint for the physical body, and eventually ulcers may develop. Although you may be very aware of the ulcer in the physical body, you may not be aware that the ulcer is also present as an energetic pattern in the etheric body, and that the ulcer's energetic pattern was created by the anger in the emotional body, and that the anger is your reaction to the thought form "I am unworthy of . . ." in the mental body.

Developing Sensitivity to Energy

"The Laser" and "The Hand Bounce" are two easy exercises one can do to develop the ability to detect and "feel" energy. While doing these exercises, be very aware of any differences between your hands in the way they feel or react to your energy field. It may be that only one of your hands will become sensitive to energy, and there is no way to predict which hand that may be—each person is different. In my case, my left hand is currently much more sensitive to energy fields, so I use it exclusively to scan. However, your right hand may be the sensitive one, or perhaps you are able to sense equally well with either hand. Practice the exercises below and learn for yourself how your own energy field, or that of another person, "feels" to you.

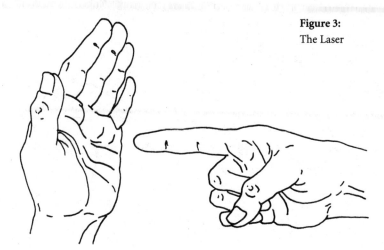

Figure 3:
The Laser

EXERCISE: THE LASER

This is a simple exercise to develop your sensitivity to energy. Curl your middle, ring, and little fingers into the palm of one hand and hold them there with the thumb and point with the extended index finger into the palm of the other hand. Move your index finger around in a circle about an inch or two away from your palm, and begin to sense the slight sense of motion across your palm. The beam of energy coming out of your moving fingertip is "slicing through" the energy field of the other hand, and you can sense this, particularly if your eyes are closed and you are concentrating on learning what that feels like. You can also move your pointing finger across the soft pad on the inside of the end joint of each finger to help develop sensitivity to energy fields in your fingertips (see Figure 3, above).

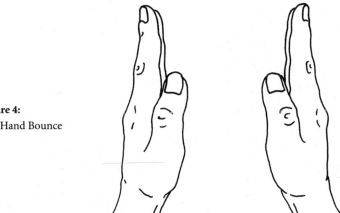

Figure 4:
The Hand Bounce

EXERCISE: THE HAND BOUNCE

Place your hands in front of you like you are going to clap them, keeping the palms about a foot apart at first (see Figure 4, above). Now begin to move your palms together until they are about three or four inches from each other, and then move them apart again to where they started. "Bounce" your hands in this way about twice a second, smoothly and continuously. Concentrate on how the palms of your hands feel. Put all your awareness into what they are sensing and how they feel to you. Now slowly start bringing your hands closer and closer together, but maintain the same eight- or nine-inch travel.

As your hands get closer, perhaps one to three inches apart from each other, you may begin to sense a very subtle, very light sense of pressure between your palms or between your fingertips. It may feel like a very gentle resistance to the movement, like trying to push soapy hands through a soap bubble. Notice this feeling and keep moving your hands steadily so you can get a stronger sense of what this feels like. Keep practicing this until you are sure that you feel something, even if you are not sure what it is.

What you feel is the energy body around your left hand meeting the energy body around your right hand. When they meet and compress each other slightly, that compression is reflected into your palms or fingertips as a slight sense of pressure. It is only at this point where the outer boundaries of the two fields meet that the pressure is felt. As you move your hands closer together, your left hand moves within the field of your right hand, and vice versa, and no pressure is felt when the field boundary of one hand is inside the field of the other hand.

Now keep moving your hands so you feel that slight sense of pressure between them, and notice your breathing. It is probably pretty shallow because you are concentrating on your hands so intently. Now begin to breathe deeply and rhythmically, and notice that your hands will have to quickly move further apart to keep feeling that same sensation between them. This is a very clear demonstration that the energy we take in through our breathing is quickly and continuously reflected into the energy fields around our bodies. In this case, the energy fields surrounding your hands expanded due to the additional energy received by deep breathing, and your hands had to move further apart to stay with that point where the boundary of the field around each hand met.

Do not be discouraged if at first you do not feel the energy fields around your hands. Keep practicing and focus on how your hands feel. Do not try to anticipate anything specific, but just keep noticing what you do feel, and practice, practice, practice!

When you are able to sense the energy field around your own hands, ask a partner to join you. Each person should use one hand and do the same "bounce" described above until you can begin to feel that same slight sensation in your palm. When you are both confident that you have the sensation with your hands a certain distance apart, have one of the partners think of something very, very sad and depressing. Notice how the distance between your hands begins to shrink a bit as you still feel that bounce or pressure in your hands. And now have them think of something very happy, loving, and energizing, and watch how their expanding field pushes your hands further apart in order to keep sensing the edge of their field. Here is proof positive that thoughts can also affect the energy levels in your aura. Perhaps you have been around someone who felt like they were draining your energy, or someone who was very positive and uplifting just to be around. What one thinks and feels is reflected in the energy bodies surrounding them, and others can sense this energy.

The Origin of Disease

For many centuries, disease was thought to be caused by evil "vapors," or spirits visiting a person's body for one reason or another. Gradually, as superstition gave way to modern investigation using the microscope, the microcosmic world began to show itself. Now with advanced equipment such as electron microscopes, we can see into the world of germs, viruses, microbes, protozoans, and parasites. To be sure, some diseases are caused by the body's inability to cope with certain bacteria, microbes, and viruses, but these are not the cause of all illnesses and diseases. Some diseases are a secondary result of traumatic injury, such as gangrene after a bone fracture. Still others seem to be caused, or at least exacerbated, by one's emotional state, such as the person who runs around angry for decades and finally develops a stomach ulcer. And there is also growing support for the idea that some diseases are developed in response to a karmic reaction so that we can learn a lesson. We will examine all these sources of disease.

Bacteria and Viruses

The ability to avoid becoming infected by unhealthy germs or viruses, and if infected, to destroy these unhealthy agents, is a measure of the health of a person's immune system. If the immune system is strong, infection is checked and the self-healing process of the body is allowed to complete its work. But if the immune system is not functioning well, infection can spread and secondary complications may occur. Properly prescribed medicines and antibiotics can kill some germs and bacteria, but viruses are much more troublesome. "Allopathy (that is, traditional medicine) is clearly superb at dealing with trauma and bacterial infections. It is far less successful with asthma, chronic pain and autoimmune diseases."[13] There is still no cure for the common cold, although there are several practices that can lead to a higher resistance to catching a cold in the first place. Antioxidants such as vitamin C and E continue to be cited for having a stimulating effect on the immune system.

Your medical doctor can prescribe an effective medication to combat, for instance, strep throat. But when it comes to the treatment of diseases and symptoms that are caused by viruses, modern medicine seems lost at where to start. Arthritis, for example, is thought to be caused by a virus of some sort, and the symptoms are often treated by prescribing long-term use of steroids. However, although some symptoms may be temporarily reduced by the use of steroids, these drugs have an extremely damaging effect on a person's energy system.

I had an occasion to hand-scan the field of a person who had been using prescribed steroids for about ten years to treat arthritis. When I put my hand into her field about three or four inches from her body, my hand actually went numb from the intense vibration! Her energy system was so extremely agitated and vibrating so much and so wildly, that my own field could not analyze it and all feeling was temporarily disrupted. When I removed my hand from her field, normal sensations quickly returned. Again I put my hand into her field, and again it went numb; removing it again returned the feeling in my hand to normal. There is much we do not yet know about the body and its reactions to many chemicals and agents that are routinely prescribed to mask the symptoms of—but not actually cure—many diseases. As we learn more about the energy fields of which we are composed, we can bring this additional understanding into good use when knowledgeable medical doctors prescribe medicines for specific diseases or symptoms.

There is also a growing body of experiential evidence that a healer's application of energy stimulates the body's immune system and helps to create internal conditions that allow the person to self-heal much faster than normally would be expected. Two such healing techniques that produce this effect, Reiki and Healing Touch, are discussed in the next chapter. The use of energy-based healing techniques is becoming more and more widespread, and many Healing Touch procedures are being introduced into the recovery rooms of many of the more progressive and enlightened hospitals. Even insurance companies are beginning to compensate for the use of certain healing energy techniques simply because people get well quicker, heal with less pain, and hospital stays are shortened.

Trauma

Modern surgeons, in conjunction with modern technology, have developed an amazing ability to analyze the body's organs, blood, and tissues, and new surgical procedures are being introduced at a pace that would have been unbelievable only a few years ago. Replacement of organs and complete joints has returned many people to a healthy, fully functional lifestyle after years of crippling pain and inactivity. Surgical procedures to repair organs, tissues, and limbs, and to graft nerves, have similarly allowed many to recover the use of damaged parts of their body. The list goes on and on, and grows daily. The modern surgeon can be truly a miracle worker for the victim of a traumatic injury.

Yet there is still the chance that after all the effort on the part of the surgeon, a simple infection may develop, spread, and, unless checked, could lead to a life-threatening disease such as pneumonia, septecemia, or a host of other secondary complications. A person's ability to recover from traumatic injury and surgery is also a reflection of the health of that person's immune system to ward off infections. It is also an indication of the person's own self-healing ability to reconstruct tissues, to grow together nerves, and to construct new capillaries and blood vessels to nourish injured areas.

Each of these self-healing activities requires energy. Healing involves the process of converting the energies within the body into matter—new tissues, new blood cells, etc. Normally, the person's Human Energy Field is the energy source for the healing activity. However, regenerative healing can be significantly accelerated by applying additional energy from the Universal Energy Field, using the healer as a channel. For instance, when healing Reiki energy is applied, broken bones knit together in about one-third the normal healing time. Patients recovering from surgery require less pain relief medication after an energy-based healing technique is used. Internal bleeding can be quickly controlled, and surgical incisions tend to heal more quickly and with less scarring following energy-healing sessions.

Beliefs and Emotions

There is growing evidence that our emotional and mental health can and does affect our physical health, both positively and negatively. In her book *You Can Heal Your Life*, Louise Hay lists many diseases for which the original cause may be faulty beliefs about one's self or negative emotional reactions to what we perceive about ourselves or others.[14] For example, a person who feels stifled and suppresses crying lives in an emotional pattern that prevents that person from taking in the goodness of life. If this emotional pattern continues, it is eventually brought down into their etheric body and becomes a part of the overall pattern for the physical body, and the person may develop asthma.

Similarly, she says that AIDS, caused by a weakening of the immune system, can result when a person has faulty mental beliefs about themselves to the extent that they feel defenseless and hopeless for an extended period of time, if they have sexual guilt issues, or a strong belief in not being "good enough."

Karma

For some, the concept of past lives may be difficult to accept, and the idea that past lives could affect your current lifetime may be even harder to accept. Yet in many Eastern philosophies, the idea of incarnating in repeated lifetimes is one of the underlying foundational beliefs that permit a coherent understanding of an individual's existence and purpose. The principle of karma is simply another way of stating the Golden Rule: "Do unto others as you would have them do unto you," or "What goes around, comes around." Within the framework of karma is the expectation that everything you do is returned to you, both good and bad. Further, it is not necessary that the results of your actions be returned to you during your current lifetime; it may be delayed until a later incarnation. Karma makes sense only if viewed in the context of several lifetimes.

Another way of looking at karma is that it is a mechanism for providing us the greatest potential for our own soul growth. For example, through my free will choice I may choose to injure a person emotionally by withdrawing my love from her. Under the law of karma, I must also experience the injury that I have caused. Therefore, in a later experience, either in this lifetime or another lifetime, a situation will be created where I will be able to experience a similar withdrawal of love. In experiencing this, I am now aware of both how it feels to withdraw love and how it feels to have love withdrawn. Knowing both sides of the coin, I am now in a better position to consciously choose my future courses of action. Further, by experiencing life from all possible vantage points, I would be better able to understand all of life's complexity and beauty. "By incarnating as male and female, white and black, as Indian, Chinese, and Chicano, by experiencing life from all possible viewpoints, the reincarnational scheme allows us to see the world from all possible perspectives."[15]

However, for our discussion here, it is not necessary to believe in reincarnation or past lives. There is another very effective way of looking at our actions in a similar manner. The famous psychiatrist Carl Jung postulated the idea that all actions taken by each person on earth throughout time are recorded in what he called the "collective unconscious." He further proposed that there was some mechanism for attaching or connecting specific events in the collective unconscious with individual people. Therefore, as you choose to take a certain action, that choice and action is recorded in the collective unconscious. In addition, there is a resonance of some sort between that action and others that have already been stored, and through this resonance, these other actions are connected to your current life through your subconscious mind.

A growing number of cases from clinical hypnotherapists and regression therapists suggest that, occasionally, the original cause of a disease may be from actions taken in the past, and that those actions are now affecting their present health situation. For example, Dr. Roger Woolger, a Jungian psychotherapist, has documented several physical issues that have their origin in an earlier experience. Among these was a young woman who had suffered from ulcerative colitis. Through hypnotherapy, she relived the life of an eight-year-old Dutch girl rounded up and shot at a mass grave by Nazi soldiers. The colitis was an expression of the residual terror during the girl's last moments awaiting execution. Another was a man with chronic back pain; he relived an agonizing death pinned under a wagon with a broken back. The pain substantially lessened after the session. And still another was a woman whose chronic migraine headaches disappeared after reliving the agony of a young girl of seven; her father had killed her with a blow to the head with an iron bar.[16]

Holistic Healing of Disease Symptoms

As we become more aware of our own energetic nature and the many potential sources of diseases, it becomes more apparent that in order to effect a complete cure from disease, we must not only eliminate the symptoms of that disease (heal the physical body), but we must also eliminate the cause of the disease, which may lie in the higher energy bodies. Unless the cause of the disease is corrected, the predisposition to that disease is still there, and the disease may return.

Happily, some enlightened traditional doctors are becoming aware that in order to completely cure the disease (not just cover up, or remove, its symptoms), additional therapy beyond drugs and surgery may be necessary. Surgery may still be required, however, and can provide the patient with additional time. This time can then be used to investigate other techniques, such as Ro-Hun, which can help to repattern the higher energy bodies to a more healthy state. When the negative thoughts and beliefs one has about themselves are released (mental body), and how one reacts to and "feels" about these thoughts are brought into harmony (emotional body), these negative patterns no longer adversely affect the etheric body, the pattern for the physical body. Then and only then has the disease and its cause been completely eliminated.

In order to assist in the healing of a client's disease or symptoms, the healer must also be aware of, and sensitive to, the client's expectations and needs in a process that is much different from traditional medical treatments. Holistic healing is not just a matter of going in for a treatment and taking whatever the therapist or practitioner recommends. Instead, it involves creating a partnership for healing in which both the therapist and the client work jointly toward the goal of perfect health for the client. A strong rapport and sense of trust on the part of both is needed to prepare an effective healing program for the client. This program must address both the current physical symptoms and the cause of the symptoms, and may extend over several sessions.

How many times have you gone to a doctor and received a prescription for just one pill? Probably not very often. Similarly, energy-based healing techniques may require several sessions before positive results are seen. The number and length of sessions will be determined by the nature and duration of the illness, the overall state of health of the client, and the willingness of the client to participate actively in his or her own healing process.

Traumatic injuries, such as broken bones, burns, lacerations, etc., usually respond very quickly to energy-based healing techniques, particularly if energy healing can be begun immediately after the injury. Sometimes only a single Reiki or Healing Touch session may be required to sufficiently accelerate the healing process and speed the client back to an early recovery. But in general, three or more sessions are required to begin the client's healing and recovery process.

Longer-term or chronic illnesses usually require a longer healing program before beneficial results are assured. For example, a client who has suffered with arthritis for many years may have the pattern of swollen and painful joints locked in their etheric body as well as in their physical body, and their healing program may need to extend over several months. However, each client is different in not only their symptoms, but also the cause of their symptoms and their willingness to completely heal their illness on all levels.

I have found that the key to establishing an effective healing program for the client is a thorough initial interview that addresses not only the physical problems and symptoms, but also their emotional state, thoughts and beliefs about themselves, and their spiritual (not religious) well-being. This process of becoming acquainted with the client on all levels involves a degree of compassion, concern, and patience normally not found in a traditional doctor's interview. While the average doctor's interview lasts seven minutes, an hour or more is usually required to obtain a complete personal profile of the client.

The client's expectations of the healer are also of great importance. I have had several clients who said during the initial interview that they had heard that I had healed such-and-such a disease before, and they wanted me to heal them of the same disease. Basically, it was, "I'm sick; heal me!" In these cases, it is most important that they begin by learning how disease occurs, and how it is healed. In this process, they begin to understand that they alone are ultimately responsible for healing their disease.

Another key to an effective healing program is access to and knowledge of the energy-based healing techniques that can help the client return to total health. However in this age of specialization it is highly unusual to find a single medical doctor who is competent and qualified to repair the physical body, conduct hypnotherapy or regression sessions to remove emotional traumas and issues, enable a client to come to grips with his or her thoughts and beliefs, and attend to the spiritual needs of their patient. Few medical doctors see the need or find the time to really understand all aspects of why the person has come to them. Yet it is just this holistic approach that is necessary to return the patient to total health. This is not entirely the doctor's fault; until recently our medical schools have traditionally focused almost exclusively on either surgery or drugs to address all illnesses.

Happily this situation is rapidly changing, and now nearly all of the 125 medical universities in the United States offer elective instruction in, or at least familiarization with, a wide range of Alternative Therapies, including energy-based healing methods, acupuncture, Ayurvedic medicine, herbs and natural curatives, etc. Many hospitals are beginning to incorporate Alternative Therapy techniques such as energy-based healing into their treatment regimens simply because patients get well quicker and have fewer complications.

From the client's perspective, it is much preferable that they receive all required treatment from the practitioner they initially came to, the one with whom they have built a strong sense of trust. However, a complete holistic program for healing the client on all levels may necessarily involve a team effort where the assistance of other holistic practitioners is brought in to address the higher energy bodies.

The Client Interview

Before using any healing technique, several important considerations must be addressed. The initial session with the client should include a detailed interview which gives the healer as much information as possible about why the client has decided on energy-based healing and how to tailor an individual healing program for that client. Often, the entire first session may be devoted only to this initial interview. As a minimum, the following areas should be addressed.

Medical History

A review of the client's medical history, diagnoses, and treatments (usually either drugs or surgery) is required for the healer to get to know why the client has come to the healer. The form that I use is shown in Appendix A. The client's honesty and willingness to participate in his own healing program is essential. In particular, the healer needs to know any medications the client currently takes, and the reason or condition for which they were prescribed, and all disease symptoms the client desires to have addressed. This allows the healer to collect the information necessary for tailoring the most effective healing program for the client. It also alerts the healer to contraindications for healing sessions at that time.

If there is a history of mental illness or depression severe enough to warrant prescription of drugs or medications, the healer must be aware of this. No client with a current clinically diagnosed mental illness such as schizophrenia, psychosis, or severe delusions should be given an energy-based healing session. The reason for this is that energy work activates all energy bodies to some degree through the principle of harmonic resonance. If a disease in the physical body is to be addressed through Reiki, for example, energy patterns in the client's etheric, emotional, mental, and spiritual bodies will also be affected. If mental or emotional traumas surface in a mentally unstable client, and the client is not able to deal with these traumatic energies, serious mental damage to the client may result. Only after such conditions have been successfully treated should the healer consider accepting the person as a client. As a minimum, the energy healer should require a statement by the attending psychiatrist or clinical psychologist that the mental condition for which treatment was sought has been satisfactorily resolved.

Some forms of physical diseases, such as diabetes, require the client to take specific doses of a prescribed drug. Due to the effectiveness of energy-based healing processes, the physician who prescribed the drug should be made aware that energy-based healing techniques will be

ɪ notification to the
ɪent received before
oes not matter if the
d healing. However,
ting traditional allo-
ʋverall best interests.
The form letter that I use for this notification is shown in Appendix B. As the client's healing process continues, it is incumbent upon the client to report all physical changes noticed to their physician, and for the physician to determine if any changes to the prescribed medications are warranted.

Healing or Comfort?

Does the client want comfort from the pain and other symptoms of their disease, or do they want the disease eliminated from their entire energetic system? Does the client understand the difference between treatment of disease symptoms and holistic healing on all levels? Is she prepared and willing to participate in a holistic healing program that may affect her entire lifestyle? If comfort from pain and symptoms is all that is ready to be accepted at this point, Reiki or Healing Touch (see chapter 2) may be considered and discussed with the client. These are both very effective in repatterning the etheric and physical bodies, but often do not address the cause of the disease and its symptoms. Nevertheless, they can always safely be used to control pain and accelerate self-healing.

Why Alternative Healing?

Discuss and explore the reasons why the client has come to an energy-based alternative healer as opposed to the standard approach of seeking out a medical doctor. What have his experiences been with traditional medical doctors? Has the client had energy-based healing sessions before? If so, what techniques were used and what was the result? What was the client's reaction? Would the client consider an integrated approach using alternative and traditional medical techniques? Why or why not?

Client's Lifestyle

Review the client's lifestyle in detail. How a person feels about his relationships, home, children, job, childhood, hobbies, and likes and dislikes can significantly affect their overall health and outlook on life. What does he have or not have, do or not do, that he would be willing to change for a healthier life? What would he not be willing to change?

Why Does the Client Have this Disease?

Initiate a discussion on the specific disease condition for which they have come for healing, including their thoughts about why they have the condition. What do they believe to be the factors or reasons for disease in general, and for their own specific disease? Are they open to reasons for disease that are beyond those generally recognized by traditional medical specialists?

Why Does the Client Want to Get Well?

This may seem obvious at first—we all want to enjoy good health. But good health should not be the client's only goal. If they were well, what would they do that cannot be done now? What specific interests or activities could be pursued that cannot be enjoyed now? How will the client enjoy her health? What will the client have to change in her lifestyle if she does get well? This area is also very good for recognizing the hypochondriac who wants personalized healing attention, but who still needs to keep their real or imagined symptoms for their own identity.

Is Healing Probable?

Is the client familiar with energy-based healing to the extent that he believes or knows that he can be helped? He may have only heard of a friend who received therapeutic relief and help at the hands of a healer; in this case, he may only believe in the possibility he can be helped, too. Or he may have had a favorable previous experience with a healer; in this case, he might know that help is not only possible, but that it is probable. It is the responsibility of the healer to gain the confidence and trust of the client, and to provide an environment where positive healing results can be expected. The experienced healer who has successfully helped others with the client's condition can create a strong expectation for healing.

It is also important to note that even if healing does not occur, the client may be helped in other subtle but very important ways. For example, if a cancer patient has waited too long before coming to an alternative healer and there is no possibility remaining for the physical system to heal, most forms of energy healing can still provide relief from pain, ease of mind, and a caring, comforting environment. These are significant factors in determining the quality of life one enjoys, especially if they are approaching transition to a hospice setting.

Constructing a Holistic Healing Program

In addition to medical treatment, if required, a comprehensive healing program may include both energy-based healing techniques as well as wellness and prevention practices, including dietary changes, natural remedies, and exercise and relaxation techniques. Such a program could be constructed by discussing with the client what his personal health goals are and how much he is willing to integrate alternative health practices along with traditional medical treatments. Healing programs cannot be dictated by the healer, but must be examined, discussed, and accepted by the client with the guidance and knowledge of the healer and other holistic practitioners as required. Very rarely will one person be sufficiently versed in all alternative medical therapies that he can provide complete guidance for the client.

However, the healer should be knowledgeable in a variety of energy-based healing techniques to formulate an appropriate healing program based on the physical, emotional, mental, and spiritual needs of the client. If the client wants only comfort from pain, a series of Reiki or Healing Touch sessions may be warranted. If a truly holistic healing program is desired and the client is mentally and emotionally ready for it, Reiki or Healing Touch may be indicated initially to alleviate the immediate symptoms of pain. This could then be followed by a series of, for example, Spiritual Surgery sessions to ensure that the energetic pattern of the diseased organ or tissue is replaced with a healthy organ. This new, healthy energy pattern will soon be reflected from the etheric body into the physical body for a temporary "cure."

For the greatest assurance that the disease or symptoms will not recur, a series of Ro-Hun sessions may be required to remove the cause of the disease in the Emotional/Mental bodies (see chapter 4). Finally, and only if the client has sufficiently prepared themselves, the Spiritual Body may be awakened so that the client begins to remember who he really is, why he is here experiencing these situations, and what is the true purpose of the situations.

The true purpose of all energy-based healing is spiritual awakening. Many clients will not be ready for such a comprehensive and life-changing program, and will elect to address only those parts of it that they can incorporate into their daily life at that time. Nevertheless, the seeds will have been planted in the client's awareness, and they will flourish and bloom in their own time. The truly holistic energy healer must be prepared to either offer techniques which address each of the five energy layers of the Human Energy Field (physical, etheric, emotional, mental, and spiritual), or must know other healers who can participate in the client's overall program.

To form a complete holistic energy-based healing program, the healer and client need to agree on what needs to be done and what the client is willing to do. Depending on the disease, the program may, for example, start with a series of three Healing Touch sessions on Monday, Wednesday, and Friday to repattern the etheric template, and be immediately followed by Reiki sessions to accelerate healing and stimulate the autoimmune system. Additional Healing Touch sessions may be scheduled until positive physical changes are seen. With satisfactory healing of the physical and etheric energy bodies, attention can then be turned to the emotional and mental energy bodies to discover and eliminate the cause of the disease. A Ro-Hun Purification series of three sessions may be agreed upon to begin this process, with additional Ro-Hun sessions as desired. If the client desires and is properly prepared, the energy-healing program may conclude with one or more Light Energization sessions. Additional lifestyle changes such as diet and exercise may also be warranted. Depending on the client's desires and prior experiences, naturopathic or homeopathic therapies may also be recommended.

Obviously, the above sample healing program may need modification, depending on the client's needs. However, it illustrates that all energy bodies of the Human Energy Field must be addressed to ensure that both the disease symptoms and the cause of the disease have been eliminated forever. In addition to this energy-based healing approach, the client may also be referred to the proper specialists for follow-up lifestyle improvements (such as diet, exercise, meditation, yoga, etc.) that the client desires. It is unlikely that any single alternative healer will be able to provide all the services required in a thorough and comprehensive healing program. Therefore, each holistic healer should maintain a network of contacts to which the client may be referred for those modalities not practiced by himself. Once the client is returned to a state of health on all energy levels, the new healing program and lifestyle changes will allow the client to live in a disease-prevention consciousness, rather than in a disease-correction mode.

Healing Preparations

As one continues to experience the healing energies transferred during a session, the healer cannot help but become very aware that there is a great amount of unseen help and assistance available to call upon. The initial hope and faith that this spiritual assistance might be there is soon replaced with a firm belief that the healer is not working alone. And then at some point, the healer may actually feel or see his spirit doctors or angels. It is at that point the healer's beliefs turn into a knowing, a personal experience which cannot be ignored or denied, that help is always available from another unseen dimension. When this knowing comes into your consciousness, there will be an automatic change in your attitudes and respect for this sacred activity of healing another person. You will quite naturally begin to take steps to ensure the sacredness of your healing sessions. You will also want to ensure that the healing area has been properly prepared, that you (the healer) are properly prepared, and that you have set a clear intent for what you want to have happen during the healing session.

Preparing the Area

In keeping with the spirit of healing, the healing area should be quiet, except perhaps for some pleasant music playing softly in the background. The area should be dimly lit, but not too dark that the client feels uncomfortable. Fluorescent lights should not be used in the healing area; the electric discharge within them produces a field that is not conducive to healing. The floor should be comfortably carpeted since the healer will probably remove their shoes during healing, and healer comfort is quite important. A massage table is ideal as a healing table for the client to lie on; in addition, a comfortable straight-backed chair should also be available if the healing modality does not require a table.

When the healing area is prepared physically, it should then be prepared energetically. This is a matter left to the preferences of each healer. But some prayer or invocation may be offered to ensure that the healing space remains sacred and that only those spirit healers who have the highest and best interests of the client at heart may enter the healing space to work with and through you. Each healer will develop his or her own prayer of purification that conforms to his or her own beliefs and practices. A typical invocation that I use is: "Father/Mother/Creator, I ask that you bless this healing area as a place of holy and sacred connection between us. I ask that you surround this healing area with your white light protection so that only those who are in Service to the Light, and are from the Throne of Grace, may approach this healing table. So be it! Amen."

Preparing the Healer

The healer should approach the healing table and the client only after thoroughly centering and preparing him energetically for the healing session. This preparation often includes a meditation to bring up and align the healing energies within the healer's energy system. There are many excellent meditations or guided visualizations for this. One of my favorites is the Hara Alignment, which is described by Barbara Brennan in her second book, *Light Emerging*. This particular meditation connects your internal energy centers with the energies of Mother Earth below and the Universal Heavens above. When the energies from above and below are allowed to come into your body, blend in your heart, and flow down into your arms and hands, the healer becomes a channel through which these energies can freely flow into the client to stimulate and accelerate his own healing process.[17]

Setting Your Intent

After the area has been energetically prepared and the healer has been centered, only then should the client be approached and the healing session begun. The healer should begin the healing session by consciously stating (preferably aloud) their intent for the session. It is very important that both the healer and the client understand and agree that the healer's intent should not be to heal the client, and the client's intent should not be that the healer heal him or her (see "Taking Responsibility for Healing" below). The healer's intent should always be the same for each healing session: to be a clear and open channel for the healing energies so that they may be given for the client's highest and best good at that time. The client's intent should be to graciously accept the gift of these healing energies, and to use them for their own highest and best good at that time.

An opening prayer which states the healer's intent is always a good way to begin a healing session if the client does not object. One that I use regularly is: "Mother/Father/Creator, I ask to be used as a clear and open channel of love, light, and healing for _____ (name) as we move into a (healing, Reiki, Ro-Hun, Bioenergy, etc.) session. Father, use me, use me, use me. I call on my spirit doctors, guides, and angels, and _____(name)'s spirit doctors, guides, and angels to be present and assist in this healing. And I ask that all healing energies coming through be for the highest and best good of all concerned at this time, and in Divine order. So Be It!"

Developing a Trusting Healer-Client Relationship

The relationship between the healer and the client must be based on mutual respect and trust. It must become a partnership for the purpose of healing. If the client is not convinced that the healer has only their best interests at heart, they will put up energetic blocks and resistance to the healing energies. The old adage: "You can lead a horse to water, but you cannot make him drink," is still true. The healer can go through all sorts of ritual preparations and invocations, but if the client is not comfortable with the healer, the healing session probably will not be as effective as it could otherwise be.

For this reason, it is very important that when the client meets the healer for the first time, the healer should take whatever time is required to answer any questions the client may have. This includes questions about what healing techniques are available for the client's symptoms, why one technique is recommended over the others, and what that technique entails. When the client feels confident that the healer knows what he is talking about, a strong basis for trust in the healer can be developed on the part of the client.

The client must also trust in the healing process itself. If the healer can provide clear information regarding the use of the recommended technique in prior similar cases, strong confidence in that healing technique can also be developed. However, if the client does not believe that the healing session will be effective, it probably will not be. This negative belief or block on the part of the client may prevent the offered healing energies from being accepted by the client. The subconscious mind of the client must believe that the energies will help the client's overall condition before it will agree to accept them into the client's energy system.

The client's subconscious mind is always in charge of accepting or rejecting healing energies based on "Are these energies in my overall best interests at this time?" One who believes in the effectiveness of the healing process, whatever it is (energy work, pills, physical therapy, etc.), and who wants to release the disease or its symptoms, may readily accept the healing energies offered by the therapist. However, a hypochondriac whose identity requires a certain set of symptoms will nearly always reject the healing energies. To accept them and lose the symptoms may cause them to lose their identity, and this wouldn't be "allowed" by the subconscious mind.

Taking Responsibility for Healing

The person who always says, "I'm a healer; I can heal you" is only fooling himself and is trying to fool others as well. One of the more difficult concepts for some to accept is that each person is ultimately responsible for healing themselves. Occasionally, I will get a client who says, "You're a healer—heal me of my disease!" The first thing that has to happen in a case like this is a little reeducation on the part of the client. Because the client's Higher Self is always in charge of accepting or rejecting healing energies, the client is always ultimately responsible for his own healing. The healer can make the healing energy available, but it is the client who accepts or rejects it, and makes use of this energy to heal a disease or alleviate symptoms within his own body.

Similarly, a medical doctor does not heal a patient when he or she prescribes a certain drug; the drug can only create more favorable conditions in the patient so he can heal himself. Nor does a surgeon heal a patient when he removes a diseased organ. But with surgery, the patient may be able to self-heal more quickly than with the diseased organ. If healing energy is accepted consciously by the client ("I want to be healed") and subconsciously ("Healing is in my best interests at this time"), it will always be directed through his internal energy distribution system, the meridians, to where it is most needed. This healing energy can significantly accelerate the client's own healing process, whether or not surgery or drugs were involved.

Because it is the client who is responsible for his own healing, the energy healer should never have any preconceived expectations or anticipated outcomes for the healing session. In the great majority of cases where the client consciously wants to accept the healing energies and the healer is properly prepared, an effective healing session will be held. However, there may be cases when a physical healing is not in the highest and best interests of the client at that time. The client's subconscious mind may have agreed to experience a certain disease in order to learn a lesson. If that lesson has not yet been learned, the disease and its symptoms are still required until the client "gets it" on a conscious level. The high-powered Type-A executive who lives in a mental pressure cooker may develop ulcers unless he learns to balance his time, activities, and emotions.

As therapists become more intuitive, they begin to ask, "Why does the client have this disease? What is the underlying cause of these symptoms?" As we begin to examine more and more cases using hypnotherapy, regression therapy, or Ro-Hun, we begin to uncover a recurring pattern. The client's soul may have agreed to experience a certain disease or set of symptoms because in the past the client's soul was responsible for causing the same or similar set of symptoms in someone else. The client must always follow the Universal Law of Cause and Effect.

Figure 5a:
Healer (left) and
Client (right)

Figure 5b:
Healer (left) connected
with Client's energy
field (right)

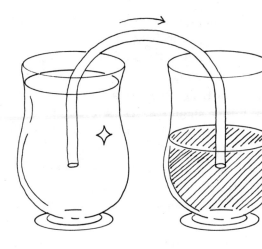

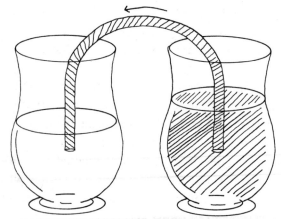

Figure 5c:
Healer's energy level
(left) lower than
Client's (right)

Protecting Your Own Energy Field

The energy coming from a healer's hands must originate in one of two places: the healer's own Human Energy Field (HEF) or the Universal Energy Field (UEF). The ideal situation is to be an open channel for energy from the UEF so that your own HEF is not drawn upon or depleted. This is why it is important for the healer to properly prepare and open himself as a channel for that energy. The healer may also be energetically opened as a channel of universal energy through an initiation process into the energy of certain symbols (see "Reiki" in chapter 2).

However, if the healer is not so opened and is not properly centered and prepared, his own HEF will be used as the source of healing energy. This is acceptable as long as the healer's HEF is constantly replenished so that it does not become depleted. The easiest way to maintain an energetically full HEF is simply to breathe deeply. The breath and our chakra system are our normal ways of taking in energy from the UEF. As we breathe more deeply, we take in more energy and our own HEF becomes stronger, as shown in the previous exercises for breathing deeply while doing the Hand Bounce exercise to develop sensitivity to energy fields.

If the healer relies on his own HEF for healing energy, and does not breathe deeply while transferring energy to a client, the healer's own HEF will become depleted after awhile. This will make the healer more physically tired, less mentally alert, and more emotionally reactive. In this situation, it is also entirely possible for the healer to begin taking on some of the client's symptoms, aches, and pains! Exactly this situation has been the source of much concern and discussion, particularly by many nurses in several Healing Touch workshops I have attended.

To understand clearly what's going on in this situation, consider the energy fields of a healer and a client when the healer has not yet moved into the client's energy field (that is, is still several feet away). Referring to Figure 5a (see page 42), the glasses on the left and right represent the energy system of the client and healer, respectively. The healer's energy level is very high, and is represented by the high level of clear water in his glass. However, the client's energy level is lower and is cloudy, due to the effects of the disease and symptoms experienced. Now in Figure 5b, when the healer intentionally enters the field of the client, healing energy can flow from his high-level energy system to the low-energy system of the client through the "siphon" connecting their two fields. If the client accepts the healing energy, physical healing can occur.

But what happens if the healer is having a bad day, or if the healer is a nurse who is physically exhausted at the end of a 12-hour shift? As shown in Figure 5c, the healer's energy level may be lower than that of the client, and energy will flow, just like water through the siphon, from a point of higher energy (the client) to a point of lower energy (the healer). The pain felt by sick or injured patients has often been transferred to attending nurses in this situation, and this pain is often reflected into the same area of the nurse's body. For instance, a patient recovering from hip replacement surgery may inadvertently transfer his trauma and pain into the same hip area of the attending nurse. If the nurse is not aware of the energetic balancing act in this situation, she may be very surprised or shocked, and wonder, "What is going on here? Why does my hip hurt?" But if she understands what is causing these sensations, she can quickly and easily replenish her own energy field with some deep yogic breathing.

Healing the
Physical Energy Body

Treatment is directed at the reduction and elimination of symptoms, and infrequently at actual cure; healing is directed at mobilizing the mind and body to enhance the natural defenses, accelerate recovery from illness, and promote full health.

—Elliott S. Dacher, M.D. *Psychoneuroimmunology,*
The New Mind/Body Healing Program

There are many techniques which fall under the umbrella of energy-based healing and which have physical healing as one of their goals. We cannot look at all of them in depth in one chapter, but I have selected two for a closer look. The first, Reiki, uses physical touch similar to "laying-on of hands" to transfer healing energy through the healer directly to the client's physical body. The second, Healing Touch, uses a combination of procedures that involve physical touch, manipulation of the subtle energy bodies surrounding the physical body, or both. Reiki and Healing Touch both provide very impressive physical healing capabilities. Both techniques are easy to learn and practice, don't depend on any detailed knowledge of the human anatomy, are easy to administer nearly anywhere, and don't require any tools or instruments other than your own hands.

Reiki

Reiki is a Japanese word which means "Light" (*rei*) and "Universal Life Force Energy" (*ki*). In other cultures this life-force energy is called *chi* (China) or *prana* (India). The Reiki healing energy is transferred to the client through the healer's hands, which are placed directly on the body or clothing of the client. A typical Reiki healing session is conducted with the client lying down on a healing table. The healer's hands are placed in a series of static positions on the client's body. The healer holds them motionless for a few minutes, and then moves to another position on the client's body. A full Reiki healing session usually lasts between forty-five minutes to one hour.

Reiki energy is always safe for the client, and will only accelerate the return of damaged cells or weakened systems to a state of natural health. Furthermore, this energy cannot be "overdosed." If a healer continues to make Reiki energy available after the body no longer needs it, the client's Higher Self will automatically stop accepting the energy. The healing energy also flows easily through blankets, clothing, and even plaster casts.

Reiki is an excellent healing technique to use in the case of traumatic injuries such as lacerations, bruises, broken bones, healing of operative incisions, etc. Reiki energy can significantly accelerate the body's own healing processes and strengthen the immune system to further protect against secondary infection and disease. Broken bones heal significantly faster when Reiki is applied. However, be sure that the broken bone is correctly set and immobilized before applying Reiki; otherwise, the bone cells may quickly begin to regenerate in the wrong position.

The number of Reiki sessions that would be required would depend on the nature of the client's symptoms and how long they have persisted. Traumatic injuries respond quite effectively with just one session, or one session on each of two successive days. However, chronic conditions or symptoms may require many sessions over an extended period. In this case, a good rule of thumb is to provide a Reiki session every other day for four or five days, and then once a week until the symptoms abate.

Long-term use of Reiki for a specific individual should be considered as complementary to care and treatment provided by traditional doctors. The doctor should be made aware that Reiki sessions are being provided, even if he or she does not believe in their effectiveness. As mentioned earlier, this is particularly true where the client's symptoms include hormonal or chemical imbalances in the body (e.g., diabetes, anemia, etc.) for which they are currently taking medication. The licensed physician should closely monitor the patient's condition while Reiki sessions are being provided, so that any changes to prescribed medications can be made.

Reiki energy can also be effectively used to aid in the release of harmful toxins within the physical body. A Reiki session on each of four successive days will move the energies within the body to release many built-up toxins. It is essential that the client drink at least two quarts of water—preferably distilled—each day during this detoxification process to eliminate the toxins from the body. It is also possible that minor temporary side effects (e.g., headache, nausea, perspiring, etc.) may be experienced during this intensive Reiki regimen.

Reiki is a universal energy which promotes only healthy growth, and this energy can be transferred to and used by all living things—people, animals, plants, and trees. Veterinarians are beginning to recognize that Reiki energy significantly accelerates the healing processes in both large and small animals. Horticulturists and gardeners are able to raise larger, healthier flowers, vegetables, and fruits through the use of Reiki on their plants and trees. This is clear testimony that Reiki is a very powerful universal life-force energy.

History of Reiki

Reiki is one of the forms of healing that was given to Buddha upon his enlightenment some 2,500 years ago. When he taught his students how to heal using this technique, they documented the procedures in a Sanskrit manuscript. Included in the text were several symbols that were to be used, but how they were to be used was not included. A Japanese scholar, Dr. Mikao Usui, rediscovered these ancient texts in the late nineteenth century. Eventually, during a transcendental meditation, the complete knowledge of each symbol and how it was to be used was made known to Dr. Usui, who then called this form of healing "Reiki."

As Dr. Usui continued his healing practice near Tokyo, his fame as a healer of all diseases quickly spread through the countryside. At one point he was called to the emperor's palace in Tokyo to heal the emperor's son, who was critically ill, and for whom all physicians gave no hope. The emperor's son returned to complete health in a matter of days, and the emperor immediately declared Reiki and Dr. Usui Japanese national treasures. This meant that the healing process was to remain secret, never be given to an outsider, and the knowledge of Reiki was never to leave the shores of Japan.

Just prior to Dr. Usui's death in 1926, he gave all knowledge of Reiki to his young successor, Dr. Hayashi, who had been working in his clinic for several years. In the late 1930s, Dr. Hayashi clairvoyantly foresaw the impending war with the United States and also its outcome. In order to ensure that the practice of Reiki would not be lost upon the destruction of Japan, he passed most Reiki knowledge to a Japanese-American living in Hawaii, Mrs. Hawayo Takata. Due to the widespread destruction in Japan during the Second World War, it is assumed that all prior written knowledge of the Reiki secrets, including the recovered Sanskrit manuscript, have been lost forever. Until recently, most of what is known of Reiki today has been passed down verbally from Mrs. Takata and her students.

Central to the technique of Reiki is the idea that certain universal symbols have been given the capability to heal the physical body; that is, these symbols contain healing energy themselves. And when properly applied to the body of another, this healing energy is given as a gift from the universe to that individual to promote his or her healing. For many centuries, these symbols were closely guarded as sacred secrets, and had been preserved for generations in certain Tibetan Buddhist monasteries.

However, in modern times as we begin to sense a quickening in the consciousness of humankind, these secrets have been allowed to come into the open for inspection and understanding. If you go to your local bookstore, you might find several books on Reiki, some of which even include the symbols. But just knowing what a symbol looks like does not give one the ability to use it for any purpose. One must be initiated into the *energy* of each symbol during an attunement or initiation ceremony. In other words, you cannot give what you have not received. When the energy of the symbol has been placed into the energy system of an individual, that person is then—and only then—

able to use the energy of that symbol, and it can be used only for healing purposes.

Mrs. Takata initiated her students into three levels of Reiki: A Level I initiation allows the Reiki practitioner to heal others by placing their hands on the client. However, they did not need, nor were they given, any conscious knowledge of the symbols. The Level I attunement session also includes training and practice in the hand positions to be used for healing sessions. The attunement for Level II (Advanced Reiki practitioner) provides additional symbols, which permits the practitioner to transfer or channel a higher level of healing energy than a Level I practitioner. In addition, all Level I and Level II symbols and procedures are made known to the Advanced Reiki practitioner, including those for healing people at a distance. The client receiving the healing energies does not have to be physically present with the healer. And finally, the Level III (Reiki Master) attunement provides the knowledge and energy of the Master Reiki Symbol; this enables a Level III Reiki Master to provide attunements or initiation ceremonies for all three levels.

The purpose of these progressive attunements is to gradually open the upper four chakras (Crown, Brow, Throat, and Heart) of the initiate and also to open the individual's palm chakras. This allows a great amount of healing energy from the Universal Energy Field (UEF) to enter the Reiki practitioner's Crown Chakra, pass down to and through his Heart Chakra, down his arms, and out through his palm chakras to the client.

Healing Technique

Many different individual Reiki styles or techniques are practiced, depending on the background and training of the Reiki practitioner. Although Mrs. Takata taught a specific series of hand positions to be used in a very quiet environment with no talking, some Reiki practitioners have elected to include other non-Reiki formats in their healing sessions. For instance, one Reiki practitioner uses a combination of traditional Reiki hand positions and other hand motions in a Native American environment with chanting. Another uses crystals and flower essences in conjunction with their own version of Reiki.

Many of these "alternative" Reiki practitioners may also use additional symbols that are not part of the traditional Reiki teachings.

Therefore, the person seeking a Reiki practitioner would do well to investigate not only the version of Reiki a prospective healer may use, but also inquire about the effectiveness of that Reiki practitioner's particular methods. Most reputable Reiki practitioners can arrange for a testimonial from selected previous clients with similar symptoms.

In the traditional form of Reiki taught by Mrs. Takata (and the form I practice), a typical healing session would begin by having the client remove her shoes and lie down on a healing table. It is not necessary to remove any clothing; however, large belts, buckles, necklaces, and earrings should be removed. In addition, it is a good idea to leave keys, beepers, and other metallic or electronic objects outside the healing area. After centering and attuning himself, the Reiki practitioner begins the session by placing his hands in a series of positions over the head, torso, and back of the client. Soft music in the background helps to relax the client. Practitioner comfort is quite important while practicing Reiki. A full Reiki session can easily last for forty-five minutes to an hour, and if the patient is lying on the floor, the practitioner will soon become tired from leaning over. It is much better for the client to be seated in a chair if a healing table is not available.

Each hand position is maintained for several minutes, or until the healer feels a shift in the flow of energy through his hands. This signifies that it is time to proceed to the next hand position. This shift in energy might feel like the healer's hands suddenly go from warm to cool, or it may be that a constant, slight sense of vibration ceases. The key thing the healer waits for is a change in the way his hands feel, whatever that change may be. The sensation of energy flowing through his hands is the result of the interaction of the healer's field and the client's field; therefore, the flow of energy through a healer's hands may feel quite different from client to client.

The hands are maintained in each position without any movement such as a rubbing, massage-like action or purposely vibrating or moving the hands. A gentle, light touch is all that is necessary. However, since the energy is being transferred through the palm chakras, full contact should be maintained between the healer's palms and the client's body.

The traditional series of hand positions taught by Mrs. Takata, called the "foundation series," is described below. In my Reiki healing sessions, this foundation series of hand positions is always used first, regardless of the disease or symptoms exhibited by the client. However, they may be augmented as required after the foundation series to provide Reiki energy to specific areas for which the client has symptoms, such as bursitis in the shoulder or a stomach ulcer.

It should be noted here that different Reiki practitioners might have several hand positions that are different from Mrs. Takata's foundation series. This is a matter of personal choice on the part of the Reiki practitioner. Many times the healer is intuitively guided to place his hands in a certain position. I always encourage my students to follow this intuitive guidance and trust their inner instincts. However, in the absence of any inner guidance, Takata's foundation series can always be used as a fallback or secondary option. As mentioned before, it is the Reiki attunement process, not any specific set of hand positions, that enables the Reiki practitioner to transfer healing energies to the client.

Front of Body The client should begin by lying face up on a healing table with their arms at their sides. A pillow should be placed under the back of both knees to relieve any tension on the lower part of the back. An additional pillow may be placed under the client's head if comfortable (optional). Each of the positions below should be held for three to five minutes, or until you sense a "shift" in the energy under your hands. Then go to the next hand position. The following hand positions assume that the client is lying on a healing table and is being addressed by only one Reiki practitioner.

- Eyes and Forehead

- Sides of Head

- Back of Head

- Throat Area

- Liver Area

- Spleen Area

- Upper Abdominal Area/Transverse Colon

- Lower Abdominal Area/Groin

- Heart Area

- High Heart (Thymus) Area

Back of Body At this point, ask the client to turn over on his stomach:

- Top of Spine/Occipital Ridge

- Upper Lung Area

- Main Lung Area

- Lower Lung/Diaphragm Area

- Kidneys/Adrenal Glands

- Small Intestines

- Lower Abdominal Area/Descending Colon

- Buttocks

Specifically Requested Areas (Optional) If the client has indicated a specific problem (e.g., bursitis in the shoulder, sprained ankle, laceration, or other injury anywhere), now is the time (after the full Reiki session) to provide additional energy to that specific area. Hold the area for a few minutes in any position that is comfortable for both you and the client.

Following the Reiki session, the client is often in an altered state and needs to be returned slowly to full mental clarity. Have them gently turn over again and sit on the edge of the table for a few minutes. A glass of water will help ground the client. Always discuss with your client any sensations or reactions he or she experienced while on the table. And make sure that the client is completely mentally clear before allowing them to drive.

The following example illustrates the effectiveness of Reiki on the functions of the physical body. Jane, a forty-nine-year-old female, came to me one day to receive Reiki for her diabetes and also hypnotherapy sessions for weight loss. At age twenty she had been diagnosed with

Type I diabetes and was placed on self-administered insulin injections at that time. Five years ago, she was given a small, external pump that provided a steady rate of insulin through a needle attached subcutaneously on her abdomen. During the initial interview she reported that her blood glucose (BG) levels were ranging from well below to significantly above the normal limits set by her physician (80–120). She was also required to monitor these levels every two hours while awake and supplement the dosage provided by the insulin pump as required. In addition, she stated that she had been having very erratic sleep patterns, was nearly always tired, and experienced great mood swings ranging from a feeling of depression to anger and aggressiveness. And lastly, she wanted to reduce her weight by fifty pounds to bring her weight to within the "normal" range for her height and build.

After the client interview information was taken, I suggested that hypnotherapy for weight loss should wait until her blood glucose levels had stabilized to a more normal pattern for several months; she agreed. I also advised her that, since she was currently on medication prescribed for her diabetes, I would accept her as a client only on the condition that her physician was made aware of her desire to address the diabetes with Reiki and release her unnecessary weight through hypnotherapy. Additionally, she was to regularly check with her physician to determine if any changes were needed to her prescribed medicines. I also asked Jane to keep a written record of her BG levels each time they were checked.

Upon receipt of acknowledgment of the above by Jane's physician, I began a program of weekly Reiki sessions with her, giving particular emphasis to her abdomen and pancreas area. At the time of her first Reiki session, her BG levels had been very erratic the past two weeks with swings over just a few hours from as low as 20 to well over 400. When she came for her second weekly session, the levels the past week were still ranging from 25 to 400. But by the third session, the BG level range over the previous week had been reduced from 25 to 265. At the time of the fourth session, which was held two weeks after her third session, they had further reduced and were ranging from 30 to 200. Over the next several days, but before a fifth session, her blood glucose levels were ranging from 60 to 140, a significant improvement in both the low end and high end readings. In addition, Jane reported that she now felt full of energy, could sleep soundly the whole night through, and could focus and concentrate on tasks quite easily for an extended period of time, something she could not do before. She had also lost ten pounds of excess weight on her own without the aid of hypnotherapy.

At this point, Jane and her husband moved to the Alaskan wilderness, and I was unable to continue monitoring her progress. However, during the period of the Reiki sessions, I did initiate her as an Advanced Reiki practitioner (Level II) so she could continue giving herself the healing Reiki energies.

Summary

There are two features of Reiki that tend to set this form of energy-based healing apart from others. First, the ability to transfer Reiki energy is given to a student only through an attunement or initiation process during which the energy of specific universal healing symbols is transferred into the Human Energy Field of the initiate. Secondly, the Reiki energy is transferred through a series of hand positions which concentrate on specific physical organs; the Reiki practitioner requires no knowledge of energy bodies, or the chakra system.

The first Reiki feature may at first seem a bit abstract, yet powerful physical healings have been consistently documented after a student has been "opened" or "attuned" to the energy of the Reiki symbols. No specific training or spiritual development is required of the student wishing to become a Reiki practitioner. One does not have to "be born a healer" for the attunements to be effective. Quite the contrary; many of my own Reiki students had no background or experience in healing at all. But once they found within themselves the desire to help and heal others and were led to Reiki, the Reiki attunements opened their upper chakras and palm chakras so they could effectively receive Reiki energy from the universe and transmit it to their own clients.

The second Reiki feature, that of focusing on physical organs instead of energy bodies, may be a characteristic that was determined by Dr. Usui or Mrs. Takata. It is known that the healing secrets recorded by the Buddha's students have also been passed down to modern times from teacher to student within certain Buddhist monasteries. These Buddhist monks may also have been aware of the systems of thought that include knowledge of the chakra system and the internal distribution of energy (prana) to promote healing. However, it is believed that the series of hand positions in Mrs. Takata's "foundation series" was developed either by Dr. Usui and passed on to her, or developed by Mrs. Takata herself. There is no record that Mrs. Takata's understanding of Reiki included knowledge of the subtle energy bodies; therefore, she taught her students the hand position sequence that focused only on physical organs.

With a more modern and broader perspective of energy healing and a clearer understanding of our human energetic nature, it is believed that Reiki energy is effective because the physical body and its energy template, the etheric body, are the direct recipients of the Reiki energy. Physical traumatic effects due to injuries or surgical procedures are quickly reduced and healing can be dramatically accelerated during and after a Reiki session.

However, Reiki and other forms of healing, which concentrate primarily on the physical or etheric bodies (sometimes called "Magnetic Healing"), still may not provide a permanent cure in all cases for some diseases or symptoms. Other forms of healing that are performed on the higher subtle bodies (sometimes called "Spiritual Healing") are then required to address the original cause of the disease so that a permanent cure may be provided. "Although disease may be healed at a physical/etheric level, magnetic healing may be ineffective in the long run if the ultimate cause of illness is from a higher energy level. . . . In contradistinction to magnetic healing, spiritual healing attempts to work at the level of the higher subtle bodies and chakras to effect a healing from the most primary level of disease origins. The spiritual healer works as a power source of multiple-frequency outputs to allow energy shifts at several levels simultaneously."[1]

This is not to say that Reiki is not a powerful and effective healing technique; it definitely is. However, we are now learning more about the strengths and limitations of all healing modalities, and we need to keep both sides of the coin in mind when selecting a particular technique to address a particular set of symptoms. Reiki is an excellent tool to have available in your "healing toolbox" since it is easy to administer, takes little training to become an effective healer, and can be used very effectively in a wide range of healing situations, particularly in traumatic injury or postoperative recovery situations. However, if the cause of the disease originates in the emotional or mental energy bodies, the relief provided by Reiki or other physical healing modalities may only be temporary.

Reiki training and attunements can be provided by a Reiki Master in your area. However, you probably will not find "Reiki" listed in your phone book. One way of locating a Reiki Master is to inquire at a local holistic bookstore or health center. Usually, local practitioners leave their flyers and brochures for prospective customers. Local New Age magazines or newsletters also may contain advertisements by Reiki Masters. However, care should be exercised when selecting a Reiki Master to study under, since there may be many versions of Reiki practiced in your area. It is best to ask a Reiki Master for testimonials from their students and clients. You may also find much additional information on Reiki by searching the Internet using the keyword "Reiki." An excellent website to start with can be found at www.ozemail.com.au/~tera-mai/. Others can be found in Appendix C, page 143.

Healing Touch

Healing Touch (HT) is a nonintrusive, complementary energy-based program developed through the nursing profession to clear, align, and balance the human energy system through touch. Through this realignment, the client's energy system is restored to higher levels of functioning and healing of the physical body is promoted and accelerated. The goal of HT is to restore harmony and balance in the energy system to help the person "self-heal." This is done either by a light touch to the body or by repatterning the energy field a few inches above the physical body.

Since Healing Touch is gentle and influences the whole person on all levels, it can be used on everyone, infants and elderly alike, and can take place in any setting: the home, hospitals, healing centers, accident scenes, schools, hospices, or a doctor's office.

Healing Touch is a collection of approximately thirty individual healing techniques that have been incorporated into a structured program of instruction and practice for holistic physicians, nurses, health care professionals, and lay healers. In addition, the number of healing techniques taught under Healing Touch keeps steadily increasing as the effectiveness of new techniques is proven and they are incorporated within the HT instructional program.

HT includes specific healing interventions addressing general health and well-being, stress and tension, disease prevention, grief management, pain control, neck and back problems, anxiety, wound and fracture healing, HIV/AIDS, hypertension, pre/post-surgery, headaches, migraines, cancer, arthritis, and many other diseases and symptoms.

HT is also an ideal introductory energy-based healing modality for several reasons. First, there is usually at least one HT intervention that specifically addresses most diseases or symptoms. For example, if a client comes to a HT Practitioner with a migraine headache, there is a specific intervention technique ("Pain Ridge") which has been shown to be very effective in lessening the severity of migraines.

Secondly, there is a comprehensive training program available from the beginner level to advanced levels. This program allows the student of energy-based healing to develop knowledge of the human energy system; to sense and correctly manipulate the higher energy bodies; and to develop mentally, emotionally, spiritually, and energetically with increasing knowledge of the more advanced healing techniques. The thirty or so individual techniques include several which involve physical contact with the client's body. Others involve manipulation of only the client's higher energy bodies, and some techniques include both physical contact and energy body manipulation.

Third, HT can be performed nearly anywhere, at anytime. Most HT techniques are performed with the client resting on a healing table; however, several techniques can also be performed with the client sitting in a chair. HT can also be performed very effectively on bedridden clients.

History of Healing Touch

The Healing Touch program grew out of the nursing practice of Janet Mentgen, RN, BSN, who was invited by her nursing colleagues to develop the program. Mentgen had been noticing for some time the beneficial effects many clients exhibited after having their energy field "manipulated" in various intuitively guided fashions. She began correlating certain hand movements within the patient's energy field and the results that that energy manipulation produced. Since these posi-tive effects were discernable and repeatable, she began to promote their use within her private practice, and also began to collect several individual techniques into a more formal, structured program of instruction for others.

In 1989, Healing Touch was offered as a pilot program at the University of Tennessee and in Gainsville, Florida. Because of the remarkably effective results obtained through HT, in 1990 it became a certificate program of the American Holistic Nurses' Association (AHNA)—primarily for nurses. The techniques of Healing Touch are also supported by the American Holistic Medical Association (AHMA)—primarily for holistically oriented medical doctors. The AHNA had the educational resources to develop Mentgen's material into sequenced, multilevel workshops that could be taught on weekends, or in comprehensive training sessions.

Due to its tremendous growth, the Healing Touch program soon outgrew AHNA as the certification authority for HT Practitioners for several reasons. First, the tremendously widespread popularity of HT was beginning to tax the ability of AHNA to effectively administer the program and accredit qualified HT Practitioners. Second, the HT movement had very rapidly spread worldwide and it soon became obvious that HT now clearly extended beyond the jurisdiction of the AHNA to certify HT Practitioners in other countries. Thirdly, the movement had also spread far beyond the bounds of only the nursing profession with many ministers and lay healers actively providing HT services. Therefore, a separate credentialing authority was required, and Healing Touch International, Inc. was formed in 1996.

The primary reason for formally structuring the HT program and providing a formal credentialing process was to ensure high standards and uniformity in the training of HT Practitioners. Another motive was to achieve recognition and acceptance by the professional medical and insurance communities that HT is a legitimate healing modality for which insurance payments can be authorized. When the insurance companies recognize that energy healing using HT is an effective therapeutic technique, and medical doctors are willing to prescribe such treatments where indicated, the use of energy-based healing techniques—and Healing Touch in particular—will become more widely accepted. And in many cases, energy-based healing sessions can be included in a lower-cost healing regimen than traditional allopathic therapies (drugs and surgery).

There are growing indications that many insurance companies and the medical profession are recognizing the efficacy and positive benefits of energy treatments. As of 1996, for example, Kaiser Permanente covered acupressure, acupuncture, nutrition counseling, relaxation techniques, and self-massage. Prudential Insurance covered acupuncture, biofeedback, chiropractic, massage, midwifery, and naturopathy. Many others, including Aetna U.S. Health, American National, CHAMPUS (military), CIGNA HealthCare, Guardian Life, New England Mutual Life, are now recognizing insurance claims for the growing number of alternative healing and healthcare modalities that are being practiced openly now in the U.S.[2]

Many of these alternative techniques are also being practiced as a complementary healing technique in many major hospitals. *Life* magazine featured an energy healer performing Therapeutic Touch (one of the many HT techniques) in the operating room of New York's Columbia-Presbyterian hospital during an open-heart surgery.[3] Healing Touch continues to be taught in many major hospitals to the nursing and medical staff. In January 1998 I had the opportunity to attend a class in Advanced Energy Healing Techniques held at Norfolk (Virginia) General Hospital. In addition, by 1996, many of this country's 125 medical schools, including Harvard, Yale, and Johns Hopkins, offered courses in alternative medical therapies.

Healing Touch Techniques

The thirty or so core techniques taught in HT include several which are very animated in terms of healer movements, many which are very static and slow-moving (similar to the "laying-on of hands" in Reiki), and others which are in between these two extremes. Some involve fairly complex hand movements and well-developed energetic sensitivity on the part of the healer; others are so simple that first- or second-graders can use them very effectively to help heal their own bumps, scrapes, and cuts. In addition to the healing received, another benefit of the use

HT Technique	Level	Hand Placement		Indications (Partial)
		Body	Field	
Therapeutic Touch	I	X	X	Relieve pain, stress, anxiety; accelerate healing
Ultrasound	I		X	Relieve pain, stop bleeding, accelerate healing
Magnetic Unruffle	I		X	Systemic relief, post-anesthesia, environmental sensitivities, release toxins/drugs
Scudder Technique	I	X		Arthritis, broken bones, joint problems
Hopi Technique	IIA	X		Release energy blocks in neck, back
Pain Drain	IIA	X		Release severe/chronic pain
Pain Ridge	IIA	X	X	Migraine headache, TMJ syndrome, broken bones
Etheric Unruffle	IIA	X	X	Repair energy field after trauma, operation, or childbirth
Sealing a Wound	IIB		X	Clears and vitalizes fifth layer of auric field
Lymphatic Drain	IIB		X	Cleanses/stimulates lymphatic and autoimmune systems
Spiritual Surgery	IIB	X		Repairs Etheric Template (Fifth level)

Table C: Typical Healing Touch Techniques

of the simple techniques by youngsters is to help them become aware of their own energetic makeup.

Table C, on page 60, describes a portion of the core HT techniques taught in Levels I, IIA, and IIB. The indications for selecting a particular technique run from simple stress relief through relief of acute pain, and from relief of specific disease-related symptoms to cleansing and repairing damage to the higher energy bodies.

Much of the mystery of energy healing, even in the simplest of techniques, results simply from not knowing what to do and from not understanding what is happening *energetically*. For example, the simple HT Level I technique called "Ultrasound" (no connection with the procedure for scanning inside the body with sound waves) is excellent for pain management (such as arthritic joints), for stopping bleeding, for accelerating the healing of cut or lacerated tissues, and for accelerating the healing of broken bones. Ultrasound can be administered anywhere anytime with no additional equipment or paraphernalia required. All you need is your hand and the knowledge of how to use it properly.

Simple Technique The Ultrasound procedure consists of placing the tips of the thumb, forefinger, and middle finger of one hand together and imagining or visualizing the unseen energy spike, which projects out the end of each digit for six to eight inches, being focused into a single, strong beam of energy for several inches. Now, without bending the wrist, move your whole forearm back and forth in a random motion so that your fingertips are about an inch or two above the injured area. The beam of energy projects down into the body through the injured area. If you move this beam of energy over the back of your other hand, soon you might begin to feel a faint but discernible tickling sensation as the beam of energy moves across the fine hairs.

The focused beam of energy from your fingertips is moving through the energy pattern that makes up your etheric body, and this energy interaction is felt as the light tickle. However, what happens energetically at a deeper level is that the energy beam from your moving hand is penetrating deeply within the etheric body and completely through your physical hand. This focused energy beam breaks up disturbed or blocked vibrational patterns caused by the injury. If this technique is begun immediately after a traumatic injury and continued for several minutes, the trauma to the energy pattern of the physical body will not be reflected upwards into the energy pattern of the etheric body. Pain soon subsides and a quick return to the previous healthy pattern in the physical body (accelerated healing of tissue) is promoted. Animals respond especially well to Ultrasound with immediate wound repair. Large gaping wounds woven together with Ultrasound will often shrink to a tiny scab by the next morning.[4]

Complex Technique On the other end of the spectrum, the sequence for addressing back and neck pain involves several separate processes that use both physical touch and energetic manipulation. After the client's energy system has been assessed with a pendulum and scanned using the healer's sensitized hand, the major and minor chakras are connected and balanced using a touch sequence, where the healer's hands remain static in one position for about a minute before moving to the next position. Then the client is turned over on his stomach and the minor chakras in the legs and hips are energetically connected.

This is followed by pendling each vertebra to determine if there is an energy blockage associated with that vertebra. If a blockage is found, a completely energetic technique is used next ("Open Spinal Flow") and then followed by a physical touch technique ("Vertebral Spiral Technique") which energetically connects and balances the energy flow between the autonomic and central nervous systems. If an energy blockage persists after this balancing, a technique borrowed from the Hopi Indians ("Hopi Back Technique") is nearly always effective in removing the energy block from the spine. Additional techniques such as "Repair Nerve Damage," "Pain Drain," "Ultrasound," "Laser," etc., may also be drawn upon as required.

Obviously, the back and neck procedures are complex, and the energy healer must be able to correctly assess the client's energy states and properly apply the correct HT techniques as required. This goes also for all other HT techniques, both simple and complex. In many areas of the country, there are local HT practice groups which meet weekly or biweekly to practice on each other using, over time, each HT core technique. This maintains a high state of proficiency for the HT

Practitioners and also is quite beneficial in serving as a forum to keep abreast of developments in the Healing Touch program, as well as announcing events of general interest to energy healers.

Healing Touch Educational Program

The Healing Touch program is a multilevel educational program in energy-based therapy that ranges from beginning to advanced practice.

Core HT Techniques The thirty or so core HT techniques are taught in a series of three workshops with up to twenty clock hours of experiential instruction each. As currently structured, workshops typically begin with three hours of instruction on Friday evening, and continue with nine hours of instruction on Saturday and eight hours on Sunday. Alternatively, longer sessions on Friday and Saturday can be held, with none required Friday evening. In each of the first three workshops, the student can earn fifteen to twenty Continuing Education credits.

Level I is the introductory level workshop, and is open to everyone, regardless of their background and training. The only prerequisites are a desire to help others and a strong commitment to further develop concepts and skills in energy-based therapy. In Level I the concept of the Human Energy Field (HEF) is described as it relates to modern scientific principles. The student will apply these principles as he or she learns the basic concepts and demonstrates the sequence of steps in Therapeutic Touch, an energy-based healing technique developed by Dolores Krieger and Dora Kunz. The Level I student is also taught when and how to apply eight specific intervention techniques used in HT. Each technique is taught to the students, and then the students demonstrate the technique on each other under the supervision of a trained instructor.

Level IIA workshops are provided for those who have completed Level I and now wish to increase their depth and breadth in the study of HT. This level incorporates several additional healing techniques necessary to become an advanced practitioner. Emphasis is on developing healing sequences for specific client needs. Neck and back techniques are introduced, and therapeutic interventions for specific emotional and physiological problems are discussed and practiced. Objectives at this level are to review all Level I techniques, introduce additional healing techniques, develop the healer's assessment abilities with both the pendulum and hand scan, and to develop client interviewing techniques. In addition, the student is introduced to a one-hour healing sequence for specific client problems, and given an understanding of energetic healing principles by describing specific techniques of various healers and healing modalities other than HT.

Level IIB is taught to students who have successfully completed Levels I and IIA. These workshops provide the forum to further develop the healer's Higher Sense Perception and the ability to work intuitively in response to higher guidance. Several additional advanced healing techniques are taught for working with the client's higher energy levels. Self-healing and the healer's self-development are also discussed. The student will learn and discuss advanced studies of the human energy system and perceptual tools of the healer, view healing from three separate perspectives (practitioner, client, observer), demonstrate and implement a full healing sequence, and demonstrate skill in the several advanced techniques taught.

Certification Training Level III is for students who have successfully completed Levels I, IIA and IIB and who now desire to proceed into the HT certification process and become Certified Healing Touch Practitioners. This two-segment practicum (Levels IIIA and IIIB) teaches the student how to develop and conduct a Healing Touch practice. Thirty Continuing Education credits are provided for each of the two levels. A Certified Healing Touch Practitioner (CHTP) or Instructor (CHTI) is assigned to each student as a mentor to oversee and guide the student in meeting the certification requirements. Level IIIA and IIIB workshops are conducted in a retreat setting to allow for greater centering and focus on the intense learning and practice.

Level IIIA focuses on the advanced practitioner level of HT, business concepts, ethics, client/therapist relationships, and ways to integrate activities into community healthcare programs. In addition, the student is monitored by the mentor in the application of healing techniques and healing disciplines. For certification, the student will be required, within the next year, to conduct and document one-hundred Healing Touch sessions, to demonstrate a knowledge and understanding of energetic healing principles and concepts, and to experience and describe several different healing techniques. In addition the student must document their own self-development (books read, classes attended, research and other projects participated in, etc.), and prepare a detailed case study which documents a client's progress from initial interview through therapeutic addressal of his or her condition. All documentation will be assembled into a journal for review by peers, instructors, other mentors, and eventually, the certification committee.

Level IIIB focuses on the completion of projects begun in the first segment, the intervening mentorship experience, the integration into community activities, the establishment of a healing practice, and demonstration in the expertise required for all HT healing techniques. Students will be required to describe the professional development of their healing practice, present a professional profile notebook (including a résumé), and present and discuss healing practice issues. In addition, they must present a comprehensive case study for peer review and critique, present outcomes/documentation of client sessions, discuss theories of healing, report and review the apprenticeship/mentorship process, and discuss ten other healing modalities. Upon satisfactory demonstration and performance of all requirements of Level IIIB, the student is then recommended to the HT Certification Committee that independently reviews the submitted documentation. At any stage in the Level IIIB review process, if the documentation provided is not clear or sufficiently substantive, the student will be asked to correct any deficiencies. Upon acceptance of the documentation by the HT Certification Committee, the student is officially designated as a Certified Healing Touch Practitioner (CHTP).

Instructor Training After becoming certified, the HT Practitioner can attend a Level IV workshop at which the student will be trained in the procedures to conduct Healing Touch workshops as the instructor. The emphasis here is on group dynamics, setting up programs, and principles and methods of teaching and learning. After the workshop, the instructor trainee is then required to assist another fully qualified instructor in the conduct of three Level I workshops, and then be an associate or assistant instructor in another five Level I workshops. The instructor trainee is evaluated during each of these workshops, and upon a satisfactory recommendation from all instructors, the trainee is certified as a Certified Healing Touch Instructor (CHTI) for Level I workshops only. A similar process is followed to become qualified to instruct Level IIA, IIB, IIIA, and IIIB workshops. All instructors of HT workshops are required to first become a Certified HT Instructor by Healing Touch International in order to teach the official program of Healing Touch.

Advanced Energetic Healing Techniques

Upon completion of Level IIB, the student is eligible to attend advanced Energetic Healing workshops. This is a five-part series taught by selected senior Certified Healing Touch Instructors. Each workshop provides eight to sixteen contact hours and can be taken as one- or two-day workshops, or in a shorter one-day intensive workshop. Courses are offered by Healing Touch Partnerships, Inc., throughout the United States, Canada, Australia, and New Zealand.

In Part I, Clearing the Internal Self, the student is taught more comprehensive energy system analysis methods and advanced techniques to facilitate physical, emotional, mental, and spiritual healing. In Part II, Identifying and Healing Wounds, the student learns that our lives are limited by physical, emotional, mental, or spiritual wounds that are stored energetically in the layers of our aura as a result of current, recent past, early childhood, and other lifetime experiences. The student learns how to alter the patterns so that we can be returned to who we were fully meant to be.

In Part III, the student learns how beliefs are stored energetically in one's energy field, and that they dramatically influence how we lead our lives. The student learns how to recognize limiting beliefs and how to change or release them.

The Part IV workshop teaches one how to change relationships by changing one's energy. It is based on assessing, diagnosing, and adjusting relationships between persons using the knowledge of the seven-chakra system.

In Part V, the student learns that family dynamics shape who we are, who we have become, and who we want to be. This course explores family energy patterns and shows ways to change them in a positive manner.

Healing Touch Spiritual Ministry (HTSM)

The Healing Touch Spiritual Ministry program was established in 1997 and is a continuing multilevel education program for nurses in parish and other ministry settings, and ministers in parish and pastoral ministries. It is also made available to the lay community and those who seek to explore a spiritual healing ministry involving the "laying-on of hands" and other energy-based healing therapies from a Judeo-Christian perspective. It uses an ecumenical approach combining HT techniques with prayer. Healing and anointing services are designed within the program, and every effort is made to use a particular denomination's healing rituals.

Prior to instruction in the core HT techniques described above for Levels I, IIA, and IIB, an additional introductory workshop is held before Level I. This introduction to Healing Ministry workshop is an eight-hour workshop that concentrates on related scriptures for healing work, the principles and practice of "laying-on of hands" and centering meditation. The HT Spiritual Ministry Levels I, IIA, and IIB workshops teach the same healing techniques as taught in the Healing Touch Levels I, IIA, and IIB workshops. Each HT Spiritual Ministry workshop following the introductory workshop provides fifteen to twenty contact hours of training and instruction.

HT Spiritual Ministry Level I uses a spiritual focus to teach basic intervention methods to help with specific needs. Emphasis is on personal development of those desiring to be ministers of healing. HT Spiritual Ministry Level IIA focuses on heart-centered healing and presents advanced intervention methods to help with specific healing needs. Emphasis is on models of healing within present-day church and ministry settings, and ways to integrate Healing Touch into a church or parish healing ministry. HT Spiritual Ministry Level IIB emphasizes working with spiritual guidance in being God's instrument of healing.

This program has wide appeal for nurses, especially for those in parish and hospice nursing. It is also for ministers and lay healers interested in exploring a healing ministry through the "laying-on of hands."

Those trained in HT Spiritual Ministry principles can be effectively used for church-associated healing services in administering to those in need of healing. This includes the sick, shut-ins, and those in nursing homes, hospitals, and hospices. Parish nurses, prayer teams, and clergy alike are using this work to bring about God's healing compassion.

Healing Touch for Animals (HTA)

Veterinarians for both large and small animals are now adopting energy-based healing techniques in growing numbers. This is due simply to the fact that not only humans, but animals as well, show marked improvement and accelerated healing with less pain when energetic healing techniques are used. Several HT techniques have been modified and adapted for use on animals, and other newly developed techniques have been devised to work with both small and large animals. The first formal Healing Touch for Animals workshop was held in March 1996, with a horse, a dog, a pot-bellied pig, and a small burro as the subjects. The different energy fields of the various animals were experienced and tailored techniques were devised to facilitate each animal's healing process. Periodic canine and equine workshops are regularly scheduled for small and large animals, respectively.

Healing Touch Newsletter

A sixteen-page newsletter is prepared and distributed to HT Practitioners five times each year. It contains much timely information concerning HT administration; research program progress reports; HT news from Australia, New Zealand, Canada, and other countries; and a comprehensive listing of HT, HTSM, and HTA workshops scheduled by location and workshop level. As the official news dissemination vehicle for the HT movement, it also provides timely updates on the evolving HT educational program, as well as announcing the most recent class of Certified Healing Touch Practitioners and Instructors. For further information concerning Healing Touch and its related programs, see Appendix C, page 143.

Healing the
Etheric Energy Body

The potential for a truly preventive medicine lies within a scanner that could detect illness at the etheric level prior to it becoming manifest in the physical body. By studying the etheric images representing pre-illness stages, it might be possible to utilize various types of subtle energetic therapies to correct the tendencies toward dysfunction in the system.

—Dr. Richard Gerber, *Vibrational Medicine*

Two methods of repatterning the etheric body to a state of greater physical health are discussed in this chapter. Spiritual Surgery is an advanced Healing Touch technique in which the healer takes a very passive role, opening herself to the higher spiritual healing forces available. She becomes an open channel for her work in the client's energy field. The second, Reflective Healing, involves the healer in a very interactive role through a dialogue and guided visualization with the client. Here, the healer energetically replaces diseased organs or tissues with healthy ones in the etheric body, thus allowing a healthier etheric pattern to influence the physical organs and tissues.

These are very advanced healing techniques, requiring significant training and development on the part of the healer. In particular, highly developed intuitive abilities and the ability to precisely sense and recognize energy fields are necessary. As a healer, I recognize that I must accept the responsibility for describing these procedures; however, my intent here is not to teach the reader how to perform these techniques. That can only be done by the compassionate instructors who are thoroughly qualified to teach these advanced techniques. Instead, my purpose for describing these particular techniques is to bring into the reader's awareness the knowledge of what is possible when our hearts and our minds are centered only on the client's highest and best good.

Spiritual Surgery (Healing Touch)

Several Healing Touch techniques have the goal of repatterning the Etheric Body to a vibrational state of greater health. Spiritual Surgery is one of these advanced interventions. During this technique, the healer is much less conscious of making any specific hand movements to repattern the energy field, and instead simply opens himself as an instrument of healing from the higher dimensions.

During Spiritual Surgery, the healer begins to actually experience the healing energies and forces working through him. Additionally, the healer begins to sense more of a personalization of the healing energies flowing through him. These energies are no longer strictly universal from some unseen source; instead, they now are recognized as the energies of specific higher-dimensional beings and spiritual surgeons who are working through the healer for the highest good of the client.

It is nearly impossible to describe beforehand what will be "felt" by the healer during such a healing session, simply because the healer is not in charge of who will be working through him, and how that work will be performed. The healer must instead be open and available to the healing process for which he is *but an instrument,* a link between the higher dimensions and our physical world. It may also be difficult for the reader to understand what is happening during such a healing session without a personal framework or background to give the experience direct meaning. As I recount my experience during such a session following, the reader may believe me or not believe me; however, it is only after one actually conducts such a session and experiences these sensations for himself that he will be able to know the truth of what has happened.

Each healing session is unique. What is experienced by the healer and the client is simply what is needed by the client. But it is also influenced by the client's willingness to be healed, and what the client's Higher Self is ready to accept from other sources as being in their highest and best good at that time. Nevertheless, let me describe a series of three healing sessions I conducted for a client. These sessions focused on repair of the Etheric Body, and rapid, positive results were shown in the physical body.

Nancy was a thirty-three-year-old woman who had been diagnosed by her physician with severe endometriosis seven years earlier. During my initial interview with her, she related that each period was very heavy and painful, and was also preceded by extremely painful premenstrual cramps which nearly debilitated her to the point where she could not function adequately at work. She came to me initially for Reiki sessions to help reduce the pain and help her heal. During the first Reiki session, which was about a week after the end of her period, I was guided to suggest to her that subsequent sessions include Healing Touch procedures instead of Reiki. After explaining what Healing Touch was, and what technique I would use (Spiritual Surgery), she agreed. Two Healing Touch sessions using Spiritual Surgery were conducted, two and five days respectively after the initial Reiki session.

The Spiritual Surgery technique is one where, after proper energetic preparation of the client, the healer's hands are placed on the client's body wherever the healer is intuitively guided to place them. In Nancy's case, my right hand was drawn to her Sacral Chakra, and my left hand to her Solar Plexus Chakra. As I continued to open my heart and send unconditional love to Nancy, I focused my intention on being an open channel of healing for her, and soon I felt my hands slip straight down into her abdomen. Actually, it was only my etheric hands that I felt slip into her abdomen, but the sensation was real, and it felt like my physical hands had gone into her body. In addition, I was unable to move or remove my physical hands from their positions on her body for several minutes. But since I had been trained to expect this, it seemed perfectly natural to me, and I knew this was but the first step of a miraculous healing process about to take place.

During the first Healing Touch session, my hands were literally glued to Nancy's abdomen for about fifteen minutes. Once there, I initially had no sensation or feeling in my hands at all. Near the end of the session, I began to feel several sensations in my hands, and both clairaudiently and clairvoyantly was able to observe what was happening on Nancy's higher energy levels. I had a distinct impression of continuous, soft, angelic music in the background, and in the foreground I "heard" and "saw" a medical operation being performed inside her abdomen with several instruments including scalpels, hemostats, and needle and thread. Although I observed the motion of several pairs of hands working very quickly and precisely, and saw and heard the instruments used, I did not get a clear sense of exactly what was being working on. Nevertheless, I soon "heard" a voice say very clearly: "OK. That's all for today!" Almost immediately, I felt my etheric hands withdraw from Nancy's abdomen, and my hands and arms had a distinct change in the way they felt as the spiritual surgeons withdrew. I was then able to remove my physical hands from her body and continue closing the session.

During the second Spiritual Surgery session three days later, my hands were again drawn to the Sacral and Solar Plexus Chakras, and I felt my etheric hands again drop down inside her abdomen and just rest there. As before, I was unable to move my hands from her body for several minutes. And although I continued to hear the angelic music in the background, this time I did not see an operation being performed. However, soon I clairvoyantly saw a curious, instant "video clip." A man in white coveralls with straps over his shoulders and a little white plasterer's cap was on a ladder and was using a trowel to patch up some holes in the sheetrock he was working on. He was whistling a happy little tune as he worked away filling in all the big and little holes and cracks. Soon he climbed down the ladder, picked it up, and as he walked off, he tipped his cap at me and said: "OK. We're through now! Have a good day!"

At the same time, I also had a "knowing" that this instant little "video clip" was telling me that the holes and cracks in Nancy's uterus, which had allowed the endometrium cells to enter her abdominal cavity and cause so much pain, were now all "patched up." Several weeks later, Nancy called me joyously to say that for the first time in seven years, she had not had any premenstrual cramps, and had just completed a normal, painless period.

What had actually occurred during the Healing Touch sessions was a repatterning of her Etheric Body blueprint to its original and natural state of health. This healthy vibrational pattern in her Etheric Body in turn caused the corresponding changes manifesting in her physical body, and she proceeded through a normal menstrual cycle with no pain. The "operation" that I clairvoyantly saw was the metaphor for the changes taking place in her Etheric Body.

Although I suggested a follow-up combination of Ro-Hun and Regression Therapy sessions to investigate and release the original cause of the endometriosis, Nancy was not emotionally ready to address the issues that might arise, and she then elected to terminate her healing process. I don't know whether her healing was permanent. Still, the knowledge that her symptoms had at one point been successfully addressed sent a powerful message to her confirming the effectiveness of these energy-healing techniques. Additionally, even though Nancy had terminated her healing process prior to receiving maximum benefit, the seeds of awareness of how to complete the process had been planted, and these seeds will grow when she is ready to proceed.

Reflective Healing

Reflective Healing is a technique refined and taught by Marshall Smith, codirector of Delphi University in McCaysville, Georgia. He has developed this remarkable healing process through his study and application of Spiritual Anatomy, and his extensive background and knowledge of metaphysical healing techniques gained from historical writings, more current research, and inspired guidance. This technique directly addresses the etheric body in a combination of guided imagery techniques and energy-body manipulations. The purpose of Reflective Healing is to replace the vibrational pattern of a diseased organ or tissue in the etheric body with the pattern of a normal, healthy, and perfectly functioning organ. This healthy pattern will ultimately be reflected into the physical body and replace the diseased organ or tissue.

Marshall Smith is an accomplished teacher, author, and speaker, and has done extensive biblical and comparative religion studies. He has also held a pastoral position in a nondenominational Christian church. His work in harmonizing spiritual studies with transpersonal and alternative medical therapies has resulted in a unique blend of left-brain analysis and right-brain intuitive abilities.

Smith is a retired vice-president and corporate officer of the Kimberly-Clark Corporation. He received a Bachelor of Science Degree in Electrical Engineering from the University of South Carolina, and has a doctorate in Alternative Medical Therapies, Intuitive and Spiritual Sciences, and Transpersonal Psychology.

In his studies of Spiritual Anatomy, Smith has identified four distinct layers within the etheric body; each has a specific function and purpose. The four layers are the outer Reflective Layer of the etheric body, the Light-Sensate Layer, the Life Layer, and the Chemical Layer. The Light-Sensate and Life Layers are between the outer Reflective Layer and the surface of the skin. The skin is, in fact, the Chemical Layer of the etheric body. Knowledge of these layers and their functions is combined with a guided imagery process that directly involves both therapist and client to produce changes in the client's etheric and physical energy bodies.

The guided imagery facet of this healing technique involves bringing forth the two necessary ingredients to cause physical manifestation: the thought or idea of what it is we want to create, and the deep desire and passion to bring that idea into reality. It also forces the healer to be very specific in the way the client's anatomy is addressed. The healer cannot rely on general, universal healing energies such as those provided during a Reiki session. Here, a detailed knowledge of anatomy and, in particular, the organ or system the client wants addressed, must be available to the healer so that the healing process within the client can be properly visualized and guided.

Both thought and energy/passion are absolutely necessary for anything created or changed in the physical. Without the thought, there is no direction or goal for what is created. Without the passion, we might know what we want to create, but have no desire or conviction that it would or could happen. But when the two are combined, the creative energies of the universe are brought into play and the thought quickly becomes reality. Such is the power of creative thought, and it can be used for either good or harm. In Reflective Healing, we use our energies creatively for the assistance of the client; our intentions must be pure and our hearts must be open with universal love for the client. The reflective healer must also be able to sense and selectively repattern each of the four separate layers of the etheric body.

Reflective Healing Sessions

When Reflective Healing is indicated, each session proceeds in the exact sequence discussed below. However, the specific procedures used while repatterning the etheric body will be determined by the client's needs and the organ or system being addressed during the session. Normally, a series of three Reflective Healing sessions are scheduled on each of three successive days. Each healing session is conducted with the client relaxing on a healing table, and may last from about twenty minutes to over an hour, depending on the extent and complexity of the healing required.

Relaxation of Client   After the client interview, the client is asked to remove his shoes and lie down on the healing table. The healer then talks the client through a relaxation exercise that starts at the feet and ends at the top of the head. A number of different guided exercises are available which progressively relax the client. One such exercise is to imagine a golden ball of relaxing light entering and relaxing the feet, ankles, calves, knees, etc. under the guided direction of the healer until the client's entire body is peacefully relaxing on the table.

Healer Preparation   When the client is in a relaxed state, the healer begins by moving to the client's side with his hands in an upturned position. The healer silently asks for Universal Healing Energy to come into his hands, and for the assistance of the higher dimensions as appropriate. When this energy is felt in the hands, the healer begins a specific breathing exercise to raise his own energy to the highest possible level. The healer's energy field is then expanded to totally enclose the client on the table as well as the healer.

Energize Brain Centers   Using a series of specific hand positions and motions on the client's head, healing energy is moved into the medulla and brain ventricles. This energizes and lights several energy centers within the brain, including the pineal and pituitary glands of the endocrine system. These centers are sometimes called the spiritual centers, and are closely associated with the Crown and Brow Chakras, respectively.

Scan and Repair Etheric Body The next step is to expand the volume of the client's etheric body so that its four separate layers can be individually discerned and sensed with the hand or fingers. Through intention and a specific breathing process directed at one of the client's major chakras, the client's etheric body is expanded from about an inch to about a foot or so above and around the client's physical body. This expanded etheric body is then scanned with a sensitive hand to locate any energy holes, tears, or leaks. These are areas where energy is literally pouring out of the client's energy field, and can result in pain, distress, or an overall feeling of "no energy."

These areas may be felt by various sensations in the healer's hands or fingertips; one common sensation is that of air escaping from a hole in a bicycle tube. Others include scratchiness, vibration, or a sense of hot or cold. When any disturbance in the pattern of the etheric body is detected, it is immediately repaired by placing the healer's hand directly on the client's body over the disturbance, or by placing the client's hand on the disturbance and then the healer's hand on the client's hand. Such healing techniques are also taught in Healing Touch ("Sealing a Wound").

Repattern Etheric Body After all holes, leaks, or tears have been repaired in the client's etheric body, the real work of Reflective Healing can be initiated. Using the knowledge of the function of each of the four layers of the client's etheric body (Reflective, Light-Sensate, Life, and Chemical), the healer and client enter into an interactive dialogue to visualize the perfect organ which will replace the diseased one, energetically bring it to life, and introduce it into the etheric vibrational pattern of the client. A combination of guided imagery, visualization, and specific breathing techniques are used to bring about this replacement of the organ's pattern in the etheric body. When this has been accomplished, the diseased organ in the physical body begins to realign itself with the perfect, healthy etheric blueprint.

Ground Client After the client's etheric repatterning has been completed, his overall energy field is then balanced. The client is then grounded and requested to slowly come back to full conscious awareness in a few minutes. When the client is ready, he is helped to an upright position so he can sit on the edge of the table and receive a glass of water. This helps the grounding process.

For further information on the Reflective Healing process or inquiries regarding training in Reflective Healing, see Appendix C, page 144.

Healing the Emotional and Mental Energy Bodies

The thoughts that one creates generate patterns at the mind level of nature. So we see that illness, in fact, eventually becomes manifest from the altered mind patterns through the ratchet effect—first, to effects at the etheric level and then, ultimately, at the physical level [where] we see it openly as disease.

—William Tiller, quoted by Michael Talbot
in *The Holographic Universe*

In earlier chapters, we saw that our physical health is significantly influenced by our emotional reactions to the thoughts we think and the belief systems we subscribe to. If we hold positive, uplifting thoughts as healthy vibrational patterns in our mental body, the mental body will then affect the emotional body in a constructive manner, and we "feel good" about ourselves and radiate positive, charismatic qualities in the energy of our aura. However, if we have limiting or negative beliefs or perceptions about ourselves, the vibrational pattern of our mental body causes a corresponding negative reaction in our emotional body, and we feel limited, helpless, fearful, cynical, or unworthy.

Since our mental and emotional energy fields are so closely intertwined, this chapter will deal primarily with Ro-Hun, a remarkable new healing method that specifically addresses both the mental and emotional bodies within our auric field. Ro-Hun identifies limiting or faulty thoughts in our mental body as the source cause of our negative emotional reactions and feelings. However, to highlight the strengths of Ro-Hun without a comparison to more conventional approaches for dealing with emotional problems would be telling only part of the story. Therefore, a brief discussion of the more traditional approaches for dealing with emotional issues is provided to contrast with the depth and breadth of Ro-Hun. Ro-Hun clearly goes beyond these other therapies and is much more effective in releasing the source cause of negative thoughts about self and emotional blocks held in the mental and emotional energy bodies, respectively.

Traditional Therapies

The two broad categories of traditional methods for dealing with emotional issues and mental belief systems are: Counseling and Hypnotherapy (including Regression Therapy). The capabilities and limitations of each approach are then used to formulate the requirements for the "ideal" emotional therapy.

Counseling

The process of counseling to recognize, address, and release emotional issues can be effective when the issues being dealt with are easily recognizable and manageable. In counseling, whether conducted by a social worker or a psychiatrist, the client is usually awake and alert, as opposed to being placed into an altered state. Therefore, the therapy is conducted at a *mental* level. The client is urged to talk about their own problems so that the counselor can understand the problem, identify "abnormal" behavior patterns, and recommend a potential solution.

However, there are three things in this scenario that limit the effectiveness of counseling for removal of deep emotional issues. First, the client can tell the counselor only what he is *consciously aware of.* Second, the client will tell the counselor only what the client *wants* to talk about. And third, the recommended solution usually comes from the perspective of the counselor, *not* the client. The ability to understand the surface symptoms of an emotional issue does not necessarily mean that it can be dealt with effectively through simple logic and knowledge. Further, many sessions over a period of months or years may be required, because "psychoanalytic methods of treatment, which are often slow because they fail to engage experientially and remain at an intellectual and interpretive level only."[1]

Occasionally, improper behavior may be a manifestation of some suppressed traumatic experience, and the client may not consciously be aware of the root cause of his behavior. On a purely mental or logical level, counseling and talk therapy in general just is not going to uncover the reason for this behavior. "Only a remembered trauma can be let go of."[2] Therefore, for deep emotional issues and problems, counseling alone usually provides little or no reason for changes in behavior.

Hypnotherapy

Hypnotherapy is a form of psychotherapy that directly or indirectly induces an altered state to gain access to the subconscious mind in order to alleviate subconscious conflicts and buried traumas. It is generally a very effective technique for reprogramming the subconscious mind to break old habits and substitute new ones. Smoking cessation, weight loss, removing anxiety, and building self-confidence are typical applications that usually result in positive changes in the client's behavior. If prescribed by a medical doctor, hypnotherapy may also be used effectively to treat some medical conditions such as asthma, allergies, constipation, hemorrhoids, and others.

Hypnotherapy is also very useful in dealing with some emotional problems. When the client is in an altered state, the experienced hypnotherapist can gain access to the client's subconscious memories. Memories of a traumatic experience may be too terrible to be dealt with and comprehended by the conscious mind, so they are suppressed below the threshold of consciousness. By gently guiding the client, the hypnotherapist may gain access to such memories and bring them up safely to be recognized by the conscious mind.

Hypnotherapy is a very effective tool in uncovering suppressed memories, emotions, and feelings; however, the client may only be required to understand and "forgive" the situation at only a *mental* level. The deep pain and hurt, the emotional reaction of the experience, may still affect the client's emotional energy body. He understands what happened, but it still affects the way he feels about what happened. Complete release of the underlying emotional issue can occur only when the client's energetic connection to that experience has been completely severed. Only then will that experience cease to affect his life on either a mental or emotional level.

Regression Therapy

Regression Therapy is a subspecialty of hypnotherapeutic techniques. In Regression Therapy, the client's awareness or consciousness is directed back to a point in time to fully understand the details of a past experience. The distinct difference from traditional hypnotherapy is that we may now investigate not only repressed memories from childhood, but also experiences *prior* to the client's birth. Controversial as this may seem to some, there is a rapidly growing body of knowledge and documentation dealing with experiences felt within the mother's womb prior to birth, and even with experiences prior to conception (pre-womb). Each of these is discussed below.

The Womb Experience My own work, and that of many other hypnotherapists, has convinced me that our awareness or consciousness extends back in time well before we learned the language of our parents, and could describe what was happening to, and affecting us, on our physical, emotional, and mental levels. It can be stated with certainty that human consciousness is not limited to human physical senses, nor is our capability for awareness limited by these senses. We are much, much more than what we physically perceive ourselves to be. Our awareness exists well before we are born, as evidenced by the growing number of session transcripts where clients have been regressed back to a time when they were in their mothers' wombs. These sessions are exceptionally useful in investigating and resolving emotional issues existing between a client and his or her mother or father.

For instance, a client's feelings of rejection or unworthiness may often be traced back to a womb experience where the unborn child was not wanted by the mother. The unborn child grows to term in the mother's *total energy environment,* not just her physical body. The mother's total energy field, including her mental thoughts and belief systems, as well as her emotional reactions to these beliefs, determines the energy environment in which the unborn child develops and grows. If that energy environment includes feelings of guilt, shame, or anger at being pregnant, the child within her also feels those feelings in her emotional energy field.

The unborn child has little analytical ability, since that comes after the brain is developed well after birth. Therefore, the unborn child can only receive these repeated emotional feelings of the mother and begin to incorporate them as a part of its own developing energy patterns. If the mother's thought pattern is "I don't want this child," the unborn child may begin to form an energetic mental body with the thought pattern "I am not wanted" or "I am unlovable." The unborn child has adopted the faulty thoughts and mental patterns of his mother.

> There is now a growing consensus among therapists doing deep experiential work involving prenatal and birth memories that even if the fetal infant has no ego consciousness— i.e., an identity—before or at birth, the subconscious mind of the fetus is very much awake. . . . What this means psychologically is that in the absence of an ego to discriminate, the child cannot distinguish between its own feelings or ideas and those of its mother.[3]

The unborn child's energetic emotional body may form with feelings of rejection, anger, helplessness, unworthiness, or a host of other negative reactions. It is essential to release these faulty emotional and mental patterns imprinted from our past, or from within the womb, to move ahead in the present with joy, love, balance, and harmony.

Dr. Michael Gabriel, a hypnotherapist in San Jose, California, uses four processes to investigate and heal prenatal emotional stresses and traumas: Recall, Reframing, Releasing, and Rescripting. During Recall, the client simply observes and gives words that objectively describe, but do not necessarily interpret, their pre-birth experience. During Reframing, the client calls on their adult perspective, knowledge, and experiences to give an understandable meaning to what they have described during Recall. During the Releasing process, the client releases the negative emotional connections absorbed during the pre-birth experience.

And through Rescripting, an active imagination and guided imagery process is used to relive the pre-birth experience in a positive, supporting manner. In this way, positive memories can be imprinted into the client's memories to replace the previous negative memories.[4]

Dr. Gabriel's processes are a major leap forward in the investigation, understanding, and release of negative emotional memories formed during the womb experience. These same processes can also be used in the healing of emotional issues that develop during childhood, and which may have been suppressed.

Pre-Womb Experiences During many regression cases, experiences are described which are clearly not part of the client's prenatal, childhood, or adult experience. It is clear that our awareness extends to realms or times we do not consciously consider part of our current lifetime experiences. Yet these glimpses into other dimensions are repeatedly encountered during hypnotherapeutic sessions involving regression. Therefore, we also need to be able to understand what is happening during such a regression and why, so that our rational mind can make sense of this new information and process it in a way that does not confuse us, and which aids the greater understanding of ourselves and the world we perceive.

During regression sessions where pre-womb experiences are clearly described in detail by the client, both the client and the therapist need a framework in which to understand what these experiences mean and how they relate to the client. I have conducted numerous sessions in which the client described participating in a chariot race in ancient times, or described in detail how they died at the sword of a Russian soldier hundreds of years ago, and other scenes quite vivid and real to the client. I myself have physically cried out in agony as I described in detail a scene where I was speared in the chest and died in front of my Stone Age cave. So how do we make sense of these experiences? Obviously, we must first broaden our beliefs of what we perceive as reality and how we participate in our reality. Is reincarnation real? If so, what is the reason it exists? Must I accept that concept to make sense of my world?

To answer these questions in a way that contributes to understanding the emotional and mental healing processes, we must first understand that in order to repattern our energy field so that faulty thought forms are released completely, we must first know *what* pattern is there and *why* it was created. Every thought form or belief system in our energy field is there, as a result of *some previous experience*. If a previous experi once resulted in a faulty thought and a negative emotional reaction, these can not just "go away" on their own. They will stay in your field until they are forgiven and released through some process. You created them, and only *you* can release them.

There are at least three processes that may accomplish this: Divine Forgiveness, Release through Karmic Repayment, and Release by Repatterning the Energy Bodies. Depending on your beliefs, Divine Forgiveness may be given to a person as a result of living a particularly pious or selfless life of service to others. However, a debate on the relative merits of the beliefs of different religions is not the purpose of this book. Further, I prefer to believe that our sojourn on earth is a continuing series of learning experiences, experiences where we learn of our true nature through interactions with others and, ultimately, of our own place in this universe. But the pressing questions are: "What am I supposed to learn here?" and "How does this knowledge help me understand who and what I am in my universe?"

For many centuries, Eastern philosophies that embrace the concept of reincarnation have recognized that one of the Universal Laws governing this universe is the Law of Karma, or the Law of Cause and Effect. The central truth here is that whatever you do is ultimately returned to you in kind. This is stated very succinctly in the Golden Rule: "Do unto others as you would have them do unto you." Notice, however, that it does not say that whatever you do unto others will be returned to you *in this lifetime.*

The karmic notion allows for the fact that it might not be in your best interests (i.e., for the evolvement of your highest understanding) that a negative, hurtful, or unkind act be repaid in this lifetime. To do so might interfere with the learning of the lesson you came here to learn in this lifetime. But at some point in time, you *will* be given the opportunity to experience exactly what you have previously projected into your world. That may be loving kindness, compassion and understanding, or it may be prejudice, hatred, disease, or greed. Ultimately, each person is totally accountable and responsible for his or her own situation and circumstances in life. This is determined by the nature of the previous actions and what each soul has agreed to experience in order to learn the lesson of those actions.

It is believed that many hundreds, or perhaps thousands, of lifetimes are experienced before the balancing effect of karma is erased and the soul record of earthly incarnations is cleansed to the point that the soul begins to become aware of its true nature as an evolving, spiritual being. In this earth experience, its actions in the denser third dimension reality are set into a progressive timeline from past through present to future; this permits the evolving soul to become experientially aware of the results of its actions. There is no judgment in this process at all; it is merely an opportunity for the soul to necessarily experience both sides of the coin for each of its actions, and thereby gain a greater understanding of the most productive manner in which to exercise its free will choice for subsequent actions.

Although it may be easier to explain and discuss previous life experiences in terms of reincarnation, it is, however, not absolutely necessary to *believe* in that concept. As suggested in chapter 1, if reincarnation is difficult to accept, one may think in terms of previous experiences instead of previous lives. Carl Jung, the renowned psychiatrist of the early twentieth century, theorized that all human thoughts and beliefs are somehow collected into a vast universal storehouse he called "the Collective Unconscious." Further, he taught that, at some higher level of awareness, all human consciousness is connected in a way that allows each person to access this storehouse under the right conditions. Therefore, experiences recorded by one individual in 1600 may be available to another individual in 1990, even though the reason the two lifetimes may be connected is not obvious.

However, Jung resisted the idea that these different people were separate incarnations of the same soul. Nevertheless, this Jungian philosophy allows one skeptical of reincarnation to accept the possibility of previous experiences that affect the current lifetime. Dr. Woolger takes the position that "it doesn't matter whether you believe in reincarnation or not. The unconscious mind will almost always produce a past life when invited in the right way."[5] He also continues that, "for the therapist, what is important is not the literal truth of a story but its psychological truth."[6] With this as background, it may be easier to accept and understand how to deal with the previous lives repeatedly encountered during hypnotic regression sessions.

The Ideal Emotional/Mental Therapy

The Law of Cause and Effect may require many life experiences before the soul "gets it," and has paid back all the karmic debts it has incurred to date. The ideal emotional/mental therapy should be able to shorten the number of learning experiences (lifetimes, if you accept the concept of reincarnation) required by a soul to clear its karmic slate. This would allow more enlightened choices to be made, and the soul's evolvement process would be thereby accelerated. It would permit removal of the negative energy patterns resulting from previous harmful actions, both to the client and by the client, and which have been carried forward to the present life experience. Removal of these negative patterns would enable the client to attract and enjoy an entirely new and different reality, allowing rapidly accelerated self-growth and inner awareness of his or her true nature.

The ideal emotional/mental therapy then is one that includes the use of hypnotherapeutic techniques which can access: 1) suppressed memories in the current lifetime, 2) faulty thoughts and beliefs about self which were erroneously taken on during the womb experience, and 3) previous experiences which are still affecting the client's day-to-day behavior and perception of themselves. This ideal therapy must also be capable of completely breaking and releasing for all time the energetic connections between the client and the negative experiences that have been affecting his or her life. Further, energetic repatterning of the mental and emotional bodies must be done in a way that the conscious mind understands and can rationally process. Lastly, and most importantly, all these requirements must be blended into a technique which recognizes that we are, first and foremost, truly spiritual beings who have chosen to have a human experience. This technique must also recognize our energetic nature as the framework and blueprint for what we express as our physical existence. Ro-Hun has been specifically developed as the single, comprehensive therapy to meet all these needs.

Ro-Hun Transformational Therapy

The two goals of Ro-Hun are to permanently release the negative emotional energy (your emotional issues and "baggage") from your energy field, and to awaken the intuitive and creative aspects of the client. Release of emotional issues is accomplished by a structured, yet flexible, approach that allows the client to systematically locate, identify, understand, own, forgive, and completely release all the major negative or blocked energy that may have resulted from previous emotionally traumatic experiences or faulty thoughts and belief patterns. Intuitive awakening nearly always occurs as the client progresses through the very powerful and effective transformational processes that are an integral part of the Ro-Hun sessions.

Ro-Hun is a very rapid-acting emotional healing that incorporates hypnotherapeutic techniques into a unique, spiritually oriented process of healing old emotional wounds, letting go of the negative energy in your field, and attracting positive experiences. Ro-Hun therapists all receive special training in the development of their intuitive abilities and also their ability to sense and repattern their client's energy fields. And it should also be noted that Ro-Hun, as powerful and effective as it is, is still evolving as newer and more complete processes are brought to light and refined.

The basic philosophy of Ro-Hun is that emotional issues and negative emotional energy are ultimately caused by negative or "Faulty Thought" patterns and beliefs in the mental body. Examples of faulty thoughts include "I must always be perfect;" "If I love completely, I'll be hurt;" "I'm unworthy of success and abundance;" and "I'm abandoned and am all alone." The negative emotional reactions to these faulty thoughts are stored in the emotional body and might include anger, frustration, fear, isolation, etc. The systematic Ro-Hun processes allow the client to come to terms with and release these negative thoughts in the mental body and their damaging reactions in the emotional body. By repatterning these higher energy bodies to contain more constructive, loving, and helpful patterns, there is less negativity that might subsequently affect the etheric body and ultimately the physical body. In several instances, removal of negative belief systems has caused a dramatic shift in the energy patterns in the etheric and physical bodies. In

Chakra	General Issue	Typical Faulty Thought
Root	How I See Myself	I'm not worthy of abundance.
Spleen (Sacral)	How I Feel About Myself	I'm afraid of making a mistake.
Solar Plexus	How I Think About Myself	I'm not in control of my life.
Heart	How I Care About Myself	If I love, I'll be hurt.
Throat	How I Express Myself	If I speak out, I'll be ridiculed.
Brow	How I Perceive Myself	I must always be perfect.
Crown	How I Feel About My Purpose	Life is an exercise in futility.

Table D: Chakras and Typical Faulty Thoughts

my experience, this has occasionally resulted in a complete release of physical symptoms such as pain or soreness in the lower back within a period of just a few hours or days.

The therapeutic power of Ro-Hun comes from realizing that most mental and emotional baggage is usually associated with a specific chakra. Ro-Hun provides a systematic process for locating and dealing with these chakra-related energy patterns so they can be released forever. Table D shows the general type of issues that are associated with each chakra, and an example Faulty Thought pattern that might be stored in the mental energy body near that chakra.

The Ro-Hun process addresses not only the issues in each chakra, but also the entire energetic envelope of the Human Energy Field. Although most of the initial Cleanse and Purification Table Sessions described later deal with the thought forms and energy patterns of the emotional and mental bodies, much work is also done in the higher vibrational bodies above the mental body, collectively called the Spiritual Body. In particular, the Advanced Processes bring an awareness of self as a spiritual being in a multidimensional existence. Repatterning the Spiritual, Mental, and Emotional Bodies to higher states of functioning and harmony ensures that negative influences cannot be impressed downward into the Etheric Body and ultimately manifest in the Physical Body as disease or a set of unhealthy symptoms. Therefore, Ro-Hun is a very powerful, holistic process that improves one's life on all levels.

Ro-Hun incorporates hypnotherapeutic techniques and processes in each session so that the Ro-Hun therapist can effectively guide the client to look at issues presented from the client's subconscious mind. Therefore, there are certain considerations to be observed when providing Ro-Hun or any other form of hypnotherapeutic services. First, if the potential client has previously been treated for mental illness, psychosis, or depression, it's important that a statement of satisfactory treatment of that condition be provided by the attending psychiatrist, clinical psychologist, etc., *before* the client begins any Ro-Hun sessions. Second, if the client is currently being treated for mental illness, psychosis, or depression, the Ro-Hun therapist should gently decline accepting that person as a client until the condition has been successfully treated. These precautions protect both the therapist *and* the client from situations where psychological damage might unwittingly be done by having issues arise from the client's subconscious mind that the client is not yet able to handle.

When dealing with emotional issues that are very personal and sometimes quite traumatic, it is very important for the client to understand and believe that they are not alone in this process of emotional healing. Not only is their therapist present to guide them, but also their own Higher Self is ever present to ensure that the client's emotional and mental safety is protected at all times. If the client is mentally and physically prepared, their Higher Self will always make sure that no emotional issue will surface that the client is not ready to safely face. However, on the other hand, each issue arising in a Ro-Hun session is presented by the client's subconscious mind as one which needs to be dealt with *at that time,* no matter how painful it may be to look at and work through. The client's subconscious mind completely understands what emotional baggage is present, and what parts of that baggage must be released during each session.

However, in order to completely release an emotional issue, the client must first understand the issue, and how the negative thought pattern was created in the first place. Again, only a remembered trauma can be released. Because of negative patterns in one's mental and emotional bodies, an individual's personality and outward life might reflect insecurities, fears, and assumed limitations. But if these negative patterns are removed and replaced with positive beliefs, the person's aura will then project a completely different energy quality, attracting positive experiences instead of negative ones. For instance, the faulty thought "I must always be perfect" could be replaced by "It's all right to make a mistake—that's one way of learning new things." The thought "I'm not worthy of love," could be replaced with "I have an infinite supply of love and can give and receive that love unconditionally."

When a faulty thought form is reprogrammed or transformed into a positive thought form, the effect is immediately felt in the emotional body, too. Remember that the emotional body contains the reactive emotional energy resulting from higher thoughts. Therefore, if a belief such as "I am unloved" is held in the mental body, the person may have an emotional reaction to that belief such as anger, frustration, or a feeling of worthlessness. These negative emotions are particularly powerful and cause us to act or react in ways that attract similar negative energies through the universal Law of Attraction, sometimes stated as "birds of a feather flock together."

If your emotional body is radiating anger, you will naturally attract situations that allow you to express your anger. If you radiate helplessness, you may attract situations in which you may be dominated. If you radiate unworthiness, your lifestyle can quickly become one of hardship, perhaps financially, poor health, or unfulfilling relationships. Basically, we attract what we radiate energetically from our own Human Energy Field. If our field is filled with negative emotional energies, we will have a very difficult time attracting positive, loving, empowering situations.

When a person becomes aware their own self-growth is being held back because of false beliefs and emotional baggage, a giant step has been taken toward further evolvement as a spiritual being ("ascension," if you will). However, in order to release this baggage and move forward, one must first understand not only the emotions and feelings involved (anger, hate, fear, etc.), but also *why and how* these emotional patterns came to become embedded in their energy field. All significant previous experiences that caused you to take on faulty beliefs and limiting emotional patterns must be revisited; only then can they be fully understood.

During this process of reliving an experience, the negative emotional reactions that resulted from the experience are also usually felt or relived, too. Whether that experience actually happened to you in a previous lifetime or this lifetime is not important. It is important to understand that somehow your subconscious mind has made an *energetic connection* with some previous experience. So now, that experience must be understood and released so that the energetic connection to those previous events can also be released.

Once the energetic connection to a previous set of events has been released, it can no longer influence one's energy field. At this point, or whenever a faulty thought or belief has been removed from the client's subconscious memory, a positive belief must always be substituted for the released negative one. When "I must control others to protect myself" is released, it could be replaced with "I respect the rights and ideas of others." When the negative energy of a past experience has been removed, that energy is no longer able to proceed in time and influence the current life experience. This deep emotional healing results in very powerful self-forgiveness and shifts your entire perspective to one of self-confidence and inner strength. As you shed your emotional baggage, you learn to love yourself unconditionally, become increasingly more self-confident, and begin to radiate a new sense of optimism, adventure, and inner peace, which others can sense and readily react to, even if only subconsciously.

A significant difference between Ro-Hun and the more traditional emotional therapies discussed before is that the Ro-Hun therapist receives instruction in the ability to sense and work with the energy fields surrounding the client's body. Since the vast majority of people cannot *see* energy fields, Ro-Hun therapists included, it is important to be able to sense or feel the energy field boundary layers and energy qualities with the hands. By scanning the hand through an area near a chakra but within the emotional field (as opposed to the etheric or mental fields), the therapist can detect stagnant or disturbed emotional energy patterns.

In a hypnotic state, when the client is directed to focus their attention on a chakra and describe how it "feels" to him, he may say "Like a volcano ready to explode!" or "heavy and dense" or "cold and hard." The therapist is also scanning their field at the same time to confirm what the client is saying. If the client says the chakra is "nice and clear" but the therapist feels a definite area of sluggishness, it may be that the client does not want to consciously recognize what is there. But since the client's subconscious mind has presented that sensation, it is obvious to the therapist that an issue needs to be dealt with in that particular chakra.

In addition to being sensitive to energy fields, all Ro-Hun therapists are trained in intuitive skills. Many are able to clairvoyantly see what the client sees in his mind, and to empathetically feel what the client feels. This additional source of information about the client's experience can then be used to guide the client to discover new truths about themselves. Experienced Ro-Hun therapists are both intuitive and sensitive to the client's energy field, and receive a wealth of information from the client that can be used to help guide the healing and release process.

Two basic types of Ro-Hun sessions are practiced: *Card Sessions* using a specially developed set of 177 cards, and *Table Sessions,* allowing the client to recline comfortably for an extended period of time. Each Ro-Hun Table Session usually lasts from two to two and a half hours, so client comfort is especially important. Each type of Ro-Hun session is discussed in depth below.

Card Sessions

The goal of a Ro-Hun Card Session is to locate and release the single most important emotional block holding the client back at that time from expressing his or her full potential. The Card Sessions are particularly appropriate when dealing with a specific emotional issue (e.g., "Why don't I get along well with my mother?"). Card Sessions have also been used very successfully with children as young as five or six years old. Since children this young still have very active imaginations and intuitive abilities (they have not yet learned that they are *not* intuitive), the Card Session can be turned into a "Let's Pretend" game, with excellent results.

In a typical Ro-Hun Card Session, usually lasting about an hour, the client and therapist sit side by side in comfortable chairs or on a sofa. As in the Table Sessions described later, it is important that the therapist be within the energy field of the client in order to intuitively receive additional information. A specially designed set of "Ro-Hun Therapeutic Cards" has been devised for these sessions. This deck of 177 cards has five "sets" within it: 14 Chakra Cards, 18 Self Cards, 53 Life Cards, 54 Thought Cards, and 38 Message Cards.

Since each Ro-Hun Card Session will address only one emotional block, it is necessary to first locate the particular chakra with which that issue is associated. The Chakra Card does this. There are two cards for each of the seven chakras, and each has an opposite aspect of the emotional block. For instance, the two cards for the Heart Chakra say: "The block is in your Heart Chakra, and inhibits your ability to love yourself," and "The block is in your Heart Chakra, and inhibits your relationship with others."

After each set is shuffled separately, the client draws one card face down from the Chakra Cards and turns it over. The card selected will be the one intuitively known by the client's subconscious mind that relates to the most important emotional issue that needs addressing at that time. A different card may be drawn at a later time when the emotional needs of the client have changed.

Both to illustrate what to expect in a Card Session and to demonstrate how accurate and useful they are, I will describe an actual session. Jill came to me in a very upset and disturbed frame of mind because she was in the position of having to care for her invalid mother for an extended period of time. Since her teen years, she had bitterly resented having anything to do with her mother. During the pre-session interview, I found that, as a teenager (she was now in her early sixties), Jill had wanted above anything else to become an artist. However, her mother had said, "No, you can't do that. There's no money in being an artist. Be a secretary and you can always support yourself." Jill's father also took her mother's position. After many frustrating years of trying to convince her parents she could still become an artist, she was told that if she did, she would be disowned and asked to leave the house forever. So she relented, but since then had always suppressed a deep anger at her parents for keeping her from her life's passion. She also admitted that as a result of this anger, she had become a bitter and complaining person, and was very judgmental and critical of others.

With this background we began the Card Session, and she drew the Chakra Card that said "The block is in your Brow Chakra, and causes you to judge people." As soon as she turned the card over, she saw the connection to her present personality.

The next card drawn is the Self Card. The Reactive Self Card is best explained as that aspect of your personality that is created by the emotional block, and is how you see yourself or how others see you. For example, because of a block in a chakra, you might react toward yourself or others in an angry manner, or confused manner; you may have created an Angry Self as a part of your personality because of the block, or a Confused Self, a Frightened Self, an Isolated Self, a Controlling Self, etc. When she drew and turned over the Self Card, Jill saw that it was the Complaining Self. This obviously reinforced the emerging story line as a parallel to her own situation. Up to this point her story line was "At some point you created a block in your Brow Chakra, which causes you to judge people; this resulted in the creation of an aspect of your personality where others see you as a complaining person."

The third card drawn face down by the client is the Life Card. The 53 Life Cards include various professions or family relationships that may pertain to the present life or a past life. Present Life Cards include Father, Mother, Sibling, Peer, Grandfather, Grandmother, Lover/Friend/Spouse, and the Abuser. Past Life Cards include occupations such as the Monk, Beggar, Slave, Queen, Judge, Warrior, Priestess, etc. Of the 53 Life Cards, Jill drew the Past Life Card "Artist"! Jill's story line had now become, "In some previous experience you were an Artist, and you created a block in your Brow Chakra, which causes you to judge people; this resulted in the creation of an aspect of your personality where others see you as a complaining person."

Now we know who (what character) created the block, where the block is located in Jill's energy system, and its effect on her current life.

But we still need to know *why* the block was created. All emotional blocks are caused by our reaction to the acts or ideas of ourselves or others; we then take on a faulty belief about ourselves that is not in our highest interest. After shuffling the fourth set of 54 Thought Cards, Jill drew the Faulty Thought Card: "I am unable to forgive my parents." Both fascinated and unnerved that she had drawn this specific sequence of cards, Jill began to understand her story line more completely now: "In some previous experience as an Artist, you had the Faulty Thought "I am unable to forgive my parents," and this Faulty Thought created a block in your Brow Chakra, which causes you in this lifetime to judge people. This has resulted in the creation of an aspect of your personality where others see you as a complaining person." The final piece of the puzzle to understanding and releasing the Faulty Thought and its emotional block is to learn why the Artist had that particular Faulty Thought and such a strong negative emotional reaction to that thought.

After a short induction to place the client in a relaxed state, we began working to release the Complaining Self energy, which had been made a part of her current personality. By understanding how this negative aspect of personality had been keeping her from enjoying the fullness of life, Jill was ready to release that part of her. A very specific healing process was used to accomplish this very quickly. When the Complaining Self energy had been released from her current life energy field, she was then able to be guided to "look deeper" into the more subtle energy patterns associated with previous memories which were still being held in her field.

With this preparation, we began to investigate the story line she herself had built by allowing her subconscious mind to guide the selection of each card. Since a Past Life Card had been drawn, Jill was regressed to that previous experience in which she was an Artist; we looked for the very special Artist who had the specific Faulty Thought, "I am unable to forgive my parents." Very quickly she began describing a scene in which she was a poor, starving, destitute male artist about thirty years old, and barely able to survive on the little money he made. However, being an artist was his dream, and he was not about to get a regular job, no matter what hardships he had to endure. Yet he was also very bitter about his destitute condition; he was a complaining man with no friends. He also harbored a deep hatred for his parents.

To understand how this hatred had developed, it was necessary to regress the thirty-year-old artist to an earlier time in his life before he had the Faulty Thought, "I am unable to forgive my parents." As the artist was regressed in Jill's mind, she described a scene at the kitchen table when the young boy was about ten. He was telling his parents that he had developed a real love of art and wanted to be an artist when he grew up. His mother told him, "No, you can't be an artist. They don't make any money. Be a carpenter and you can always support yourself." The lad's father also took the mother's side. We then brought the young boy forward in time a few years, and he still wanted to be an artist; by this time the tension was running very high in the family, with the parents still objecting strongly. Again the boy was progressed until he was nineteen. At that point he flatly told his parents that he was going to be an artist, regardless of what his parents thought. His parents immediately and summarily disowned him. He was told to leave the house, never return, and that they no longer considered him to be their son. Of course, he felt totally and completely abandoned, and vowed that he would never forgive them for withdrawing their love from him.

With this knowledge, Jill immediately saw not only how and why the block was created in a past lifetime, but also how that hateful emotional energy had become a part of his energy system. This negative emotional energy had not yet been addressed and released, so it had become a part of his soul record, and would continue to be brought forward with each incarnation until it had been released. The particularly powerful healing and releasing processes of Ro-Hun were then used, and Jill immediately released this negative subconscious energy pattern from the Artist's energy field in that past life. This in turn rolled forward in time into all subsequent incarnational patterns to immediately release Jill from that pattern in her current life as well. It was a profound session with deep insights for Jill, not only for uncovering and releasing her most pressing emotional block at that time, but also for an exciting, new insight about the nature of her own reality.

Following the release of the emotional block, the Ro-Hun Card Session is concluded by gently bringing the client back to full awareness, and asking them to draw a card face down from the 38 Message Cards. These cards are the "Chinese fortune cookie" of the session—a positive affirmation that the client can take home. As Jill drew the Message Card and read, "You are artistically inclined and will benefit from your hands," she nearly dropped off her chair!

As a postscript, Jill later told me that she and her mother had finally arrived at a mutually agreeable understanding and appreciation of each other. There was not total forgiveness on Jill's part of her mother's attitude and actions of nearly fifty years ago, but there was a definite acceptance of each other and a new insight into what was important to each. For even that much, Jill was very thankful for the Ro-Hun Card Session. It had at least paved the way for her to make peace with her mother in this lifetime. She has also invested in some art supplies and has begun to paint, something she had never allowed herself to do since childhood, and has found a wonderfully new creative outlet, through which she now enjoys expressing herself.

What are the odds of a particular combination of cards coming up in a single Card Session? Only 27,406,512 to 1! And then what are the odds that this particular set of five cards was drawn by the one person who needed to remove this particular emotional block and receive this particular inspirational message? Astronomical, to say the very least. Yet the unique and specific combination of cards needed by each client keeps coming up time after time. There is no doubt whatsoever in my mind that these cards, and the Ro-Hun process itself, are guided by a wisdom and intelligence from dimensions and levels of consciousness far above our normal, mundane awareness. And it continues to be a humbling experience to participate in the healing of others with the certain knowledge that such help is always available. We only have to stop and ask for it!

Table Sessions

Ro-Hun is a very rapid-acting form of emotional healing. For example, the goal in a series of three or four Ro-Hun Purification Table Sessions, held over a period of less than two weeks, is to locate and completely release forever all the major emotional victim energies and issues that are holding the client back from expressing his or her full potential.

During this "thought surgery," the mental body is energetically repatterned by removing faulty thought forms and belief systems and replacing them with positive beliefs about self, and the emotional body is repatterned for more harmonious energy flow by releasing all the negative reactive energy associated with the released faulty thoughts.

All Ro-Hun sessions except the Card Session (described previously) are conducted with the client lying comfortably on a healing table. Only the client's shoes need to be removed for a Ro-Hun session. The client is first hypnotherapeutically relaxed into a light- or medium-altered state, similar to meditation. In this state the client's conscious mind can be gently moved aside for a while to become an observer (rather than an analyzer) of the table process. However, the client will be fully aware of everything happening and consciously interacting with the Ro-Hun therapist. In this state, the therapist can access information from the client's subconscious mind without the personality and ego filters of the conscious mind coming into play.

Interaction with the client's subconscious mind is necessary for two reasons. First, the subconscious mind has access to all knowledge and experiences of the soul on the table; to the subconscious mind, it does not matter whether those previous experiences were actually from past lives of that soul or gained through some connection to the Collective Unconscious. The experiences seen by the subconscious mind are somehow relevant and are energetically connected to the current lifetime. Second, the subconscious mind has no agenda other than to protect the safety and growth of the client. All experiences are treated as real and true; it is the conscious mind that makes judgments of the reality or degree of truth that it wants to assign to an event. But once the conscious mind has made this judgment, the subconscious mind accepts that as fundamental truth and incorporates that "truth" into its greater belief systems. This is why it is so important to bypass the personality and ego agendas of the conscious mind—we need to get at those faulty beliefs embedded in the subconscious mind to remove them.

However, interaction with the client's subconscious mind has its challenges, as well as its rewards. The therapist must be well aware of the linguistic implications of each word used while the client is in a suggestive state. Obviously, a deep sense of trust between client and therapist must be established before the process is even begun, and the therapist must be specifically suited and trained to become proficient in the Ro-Hun process. It is decidedly different from many traditional therapeutic techniques that involve hypnosis. While other hypnotherapeutic techniques are mainly mental in their approach to an emotional issue and its resolution, there is a strong energetic and empathetic attunement between the Ro-Hun therapist and his client during each session. Indeed, the therapist may become so closely attuned to the client that many of the visions seen in the client's mind and feelings felt by the client are also seen and felt by the therapist. This is due, at least in part, to the development of the intuitive faculties integral to the Ro-Hun training.

From my own personal experience during the conduct of Ro-Hun Table Sessions, there is also a very strong awareness on the part of the Ro-Hun therapist that much unseen help and advice is constantly available from higher dimensions. During a smoothly flowing Ro-Hun session, the therapist may be guided to steer the conversation with the client in a particular direction without knowing why, only to find that, unknown to the therapist's conscious mind, the client's subconscious mind needed that specific question to allow a repressed, traumatic experience to be brought forward.

The second challenge that the Ro-Hun therapist has to deal with when interacting with the client's subconscious mind is that the subconscious mind does not communicate in the words of the conscious mind, but with its own *symbolic* language. The subconscious mind has access to all knowledge and information in the client's soul record—the totality of all experiences, actions, words, and thoughts of that soul— that are energetically connected to the present lifetime. However, this information is communicated to the client's conscious mind in symbolic form instead of words. The challenge for the therapist is to gently and supportively guide the client to understand what each symbol means as it comes up from the subconscious mind. Again, the words used in the interactive dialogue between client and therapist are very important, and the Ro-Hun therapist is specifically trained to guide the client to his or her own meaning and understanding of each symbol.

The systematic processes developed for Ro-Hun include the Cleanse Session, the Purification Series, the Skim Session, and the "Shadow Self" Series. In addition, several advanced processes are discussed below.

These address further transformation and integration of all aspects of your multidimensional being and realization of the abilities within your Cosmic Self. Each session is conducted using a healing table since each session will last from two to two and a half hours, and client comfort in an altered state can be maintained much more easily on a table than reclining in a chair. Additionally, with the client on a table, the therapist has convenient access to each of the client's major chakras.

Cleanse Session   The Cleanse Session is a single Table Session, which allows the curious client to experience the gentle, supporting, loving nature of Ro-Hun without getting into deep, and possibly uncomfortable, emotional trauma. Essentially, it is a good way to dip your toe into the waters of Ro-Hun to see if you want to proceed with the more in-depth Purification Series. That is not to say that the Cleanse Session is not very powerful and effective; it just deals with fewer negative issues. The essential processes within the Cleanse Session are:

- *Client Interview*—Development of an emotional/mental profile of the client.

- *Hypnotherapeutic induction* into a relaxed state of awareness.

- *The Womb Process*—Deals with and heals issues surrounding your mother and father.

- *Release Reactive Selves*—Release those aspects of your personality that make you feel unworthy, fearful, helpless, and judgmental/critical of yourself and of others.

- *Inner Child Work*—Meet your Inner Child and increase the enjoyment, fun, and spontaneity in your outer life.

- *Temple/Sanctuary Experience*—A very personal, sacred experience in the high vibrational energies of your inner being.

The Purification Series   The Purification Series is the beginning of the self-transformation process; this is where the main emotional healing work is done to release negative thought patterns and their emotional reaction from one's field. The great majority of issues dealt with here will be those where you were a victim of someone else's negative actions, and you took on a faulty thought or belief about yourself as a result. These sessions may be intense and emotional, and the client must be willing to look at issues that may be painful to address. However, remarkable benefits are received by those who do.

Usually three Table Sessions, each about two and a half hours long, are required to complete the Purification Series. The essential processes are:

- *Client Interview*—Development of an emotional/mental profile of the client.

- *Hypnotherapeutic induction* into a relaxed state of awareness.

- *The Womb Process* (first session only)—Deal with and heal issues surrounding your mother and father.

- *Male-Female Balancing*—Integrate both the analytical and intuitive aspects of self.

- *Release Reactive Selves*—Completely release feelings of unworthiness, fear, helplessness, being judgmental/critical of yourself and of others.

- *Release Emotional Issues*—Understand, forgive, and release completely the negative emotional energy associated with faulty thoughts and beliefs. These faulty thoughts and beliefs about self are then replaced with positive, empowering beliefs.

- *Inner Child Work*—Meet your Inner Child and increase the enjoyment, fun, and spontaneity in your outer life.

- *Law of Attraction*—Become comfortable with the fact that not everyone is going to like you. You only want to resonate with and attract those people and opportunities that will best allow you to express your love and your wisdom, and that will unconditionally allow you to be yourself.

- *Connect with Higher Self*—Recognize and merge with your own higher aspects.

- *Temple/Sanctuary Experience*—A very personal, sacred experience in the high vibrational energies of your inner being. Discover your purpose in this life, and meet your higher-dimensional Guides and Angels.

Skim Sessions Each Skim Session is a single Table Session lasting between two and two and a half hours. As each emotional issue is removed during the Purification Series, other issues that may be buried more deeply are then allowed to surface and are dealt with. Like peeling off layers of an onion, during each Skim Session issues are identified and removed using the same processes of the Purification Series. Skim Sessions are usually held at approximately one-month intervals after the final Purification Session and continue until all the significant issues presented are cleared.

The "Shadow Self" Series Following the full Purification Series and at least one Skim Session, the client can elect to begin the "Shadow Self" Series, sometimes called the Caged One Series. Recall that in the Purification Series discussed above, the client is releasing "victim energy" where faulty thoughts or beliefs have been adopted as a result of someone (or even themselves) abusing them in some way. In the "Shadow Self" Series, the Ro-Hun client will discover and remove faulty thoughts and emotional issues created when he was the abuser instead of the person being abused. This is the deep, dark, secret side of our psyche we refuse to admit exists. Yet each of us has that dark side, where malevolent or destructive thoughts and actions are contained in a corner of our minds below the conscious level. We purposely cage them and put them there in our subconscious mind because we do not want to admit they are a part of our being. The emotional release work done here can be as intense, or more so, than that done in the Purification Series; therefore, dealing with the abuser issues is always done after the victim issues are satisfactorily resolved in the Purification Series and Skim Sessions.

The "Shadow Self" Series usually takes four Table Sessions. The first three sessions deal with removal of the abuser energies, and with the guilt, remorse, shame, and other emotional reactions accompanying the issues. By the time the client has released her victim energies and memories (Purification and Skim Sessions), and the abuser energies and memories ("Shadow Self"), she is energetically a completely different person and radiates new and purer vibrations from all levels of her aura. The final "Shadow Self" Table Session is designed to provide a solid transition from her old views of self and the world into this new and more vibrant way of looking at, and interacting with, others and with herself. Instead of a therapeutic session to root out issues, it is a beautiful building and growing experience, using guided imagery and meditation techniques to allow the client to comfortably adjust to her exciting, new reality.

Examples of Purification Sessions

To best illustrate what to expect during a Ro-Hun Purification Session, portions of three separate sessions are described below. These illustrate how the client is gently guided to comprehend the symbolic language of the subconscious mind, and to discover his own truths on the Ro-Hun table. They also illustrate the three reasons that a scenario might be presented and described by the client during a session: to permit emotional release of negative energy associated with a previous experience, to allow experience rescripting so that the negative energetic results of a previous experience can be altered to a positive situation, and to provide inspired guidance and direction to prevent a future action that would negatively affect one's energy bodies.

Case 1: Emotional Release Sue came to me with feelings of total frustration in her life. No matter how hard she tried to be perfect and do things right, it was never enough in her eyes. She also felt that her husband was continually observing her lack of perfection, and was withdrawing emotionally from her because she was not a "perfect" wife.

In the Womb Process during the first Purification Session, I asked Sue (as an unborn child) to telepathically look into the eyes of her mother and describe her mother's thoughts and feelings. Sue said that her mother was not very loving and did not want any children. She was willing to go along with the pregnancy only because her husband wanted a child. We then regressed Sue's mother to find out why she did not want children, and discovered that when her mother was three years old, she and her two sisters had been abandoned by their mother, and were being raised by another family member. Sue's mother felt totally rejected and unloved by her mother, and had taken on the Faulty Thought "I am unloved." That pattern had become ingrained in her energy system, and now that same pattern was also becoming a part of the unborn Sue's energy environment.

When she telepathically looked into the eyes of her father, Sue initially saw a lot of love and affection for herself as an unborn baby. But when the baby was born and he saw it was a girl, Sue's father became very angry—he had very much wanted a boy to carry on the family name. The act of withdrawing his love from Sue *reinforced* her Faulty Thought "I am unloved." During Sue's childhood, the father kept pushing her to be the perfect son he never had. And when she could not measure up to his standards, he repeatedly drummed into her that she must try harder to be perfect. By regressing her father to his childhood, Sue learned that he had grown up in the same environment of being continually pushed by his father, who was not only a perfectionist, but was also cold and unloving. Sue's father had taken on his father's Faulty Thought "I must be perfect to receive love," and he was now energetically conveying that same memory on to Sue.

In this energy environment, both as an unborn child and during childhood, Sue naturally adopted these faulty thought patterns and belief systems as her own during her development, and retained them into her adulthood. During the Womb Process, however, she was guided to understand the difference between her parents' limiting beliefs and her own thoughts. She was then able to understand and forgive each parent for contributing to her faulty thoughts now. And, more importantly, she was able to forgive herself for erroneously acknowledging the beliefs of others as if they were her own beliefs. This process of forgiving herself resulted in a significant emotional release in itself.

Later, when I systematically scanned Sue's chakra system with my hand, I detected a dense field of energy surrounding her Spleen (Sacral) Chakra and began mixing the energy patterns there. I asked her to describe what she was feeling or seeing while I mixed them, but she said it felt nice and smooth to her. She obviously resisted looking at what caused the energies there, which I felt as a sharp scratchiness in the tips of my fingers. However, I knew that those energies would not have been presented unless Sue needed to deal with them at that time. I asked Sue to get in touch with *all* her feelings of resistance, and to project them out in front of her and give them form as a smaller image of herself, that resistant part of her whole personality. When I asked her to look into the eyes of her Resistant Self and describe the feelings she saw there, she began to feel fear, a fear of seeing who she really was underneath—she might not like herself! I had her surround the Resistant Self standing in front of her with light and love and slowly begin to see there was no need to fear herself.

When the Resistant Self energy was released, she was then able to look more deeply into her subconscious mind and begin to describe the symbols she saw there. Very quickly, a devil face appeared full of gloom and destruction, and was very unhappy at being discovered. As we investigated the feeling of destruction, Sue began to understand that her own self-destructive beliefs and thought patterns had been destroying her self-esteem and denying all hopes of coming to know inner happiness and joy. As I carefully guided her through this discovery, she began to understand that only she was responsible for buying into the false thoughts from her father ("I never measure up," and "I'm not good enough") and from her mother ("I'll have a hard life," and "Nothing good will ever come to me").

Then I asked Sue to visualize her mother and father (one at a time) standing in front of her as an adult, and declare to them that she understands that their faulty thought patterns have been controlling her life, and that she now intends to take back control of her life from them. With compassion, Sue was able to forgive and accept each of her parents without condoning what they had done. Then she informed each that she now knows that only she is responsible for the way she feels, and that they no longer have control over her life and her feelings. She also released back to each of them all the limiting thoughts and beliefs she had grown up with, recognizing that they were her parents' thoughts, not her own thoughts. Sue immediately had a major emotional release, and began crying great tears of joy at having taken control of her life.

However, when I rescanned the chakra with my hand, I still sensed a dense cord of energy that was leaving her Spleen Chakra and connecting to her father's Solar Plexus Chakra. I asked Sue to look down at her chakra with her mind's eye and describe what she saw there. She said it looked like "a rope coming out of her belly." When I asked her to follow the cord of energy and see where it was going, she saw it going over to her father. When I asked her which of her father's chakras it was attached to, she responded the Solar Plexus Chakra. She understood that there was still an energetic link between herself and her father that needed to be released, and that this link was from his power or control center (Solar Plexus Chakra) to her Spleen Chakra, the center of how she felt about herself. Simply understanding her father's faulty thoughts and declaring that she no longer wanted him to control her was evidently not enough to completely sever this energetic connection. What we needed was an additional process that would unquestionably communicate to Sue's subconscious mind that the energetic connection had indeed been severed.

I then asked Sue to again state her intention to the image of her father standing before her that the negative energetic connection between them be dissolved for all time. I had Sue ask her father for his participation in helping to sever this cord, and he reluctantly agreed. Then as I guided Sue to take a sharp knife and her father to put his hand on Sue's, I had them both cut the energy cord and it immediately dissipated. I then had Sue thank her father for his cooperation, and then stand tall and straight in her own energy and affirm that she and only she was now in total control of her life and her feelings. When I rescanned the chakra, it felt smooth and clear to both of us. Sue had another very positive emotional release.

Case 2: Experience Rescripting Jane came to me for Ro-Hun sessions to release many emotional issues that had been plaguing her. During the initial interview, she said that among the many issues she wanted to address was her relationship with her teenage son; he seemed to do everything possible to annoy, irritate, and anger her, for no reason that was obvious to her.

During the second Purification Session, I loosened and stirred up the energy patterns in the emotional layer above her Solar Plexus Chakra, and Jane "saw" a large, heavy box on her chest and "felt" it pressing down terribly hard and crushing the breath out of her. From her wincing grimace and labored breath, she was obviously experiencing these feelings in her mind. However, I recognized that the box was only a symbol representing something else in her subconscious mind. When I asked her to let the pain go away and to look inside the box, she saw "two round things" there. I asked her to take out the first round thing and look at it in the light so she could see what it really was. As she did so, she said it was a large wood screw about two inches long, but all of a sudden she felt it buried in her neck and she was bleeding severely. She also felt the pain in the side of her neck very clearly, so I suggested that the pain would again go away and the bleeding would stop for now, but all other details would remain very clear so we could understand them. She felt that she was dying and was very confused, upset, and angry.

Then I calmed her and asked her to look at the box on her chest again, and take out the second round thing, so we could see what it was. As she brought the round thing out into the light, she said it became a small statue of a horse-drawn chariot. I then asked her to move her awareness into the chariot, feel herself holding the reins of the chariot, and to look around and tell me what she was seeing. Immediately, she started describing a chariot race in which she was a man about twenty-two years old racing with seven other charioteers in an oval open-air amphitheater. She described in detail the smell of the dust and the sound of the horses' hooves as they raced around the course. In her mind, she was experiencing this race firsthand, and to her subconscious mind it did not matter whether it was one of her previous lives in which she incarnated as a man, or whether she connected with a remote event in someone else's life. For some reason, her subconscious mind had connected with this particular experience from the past and was now replaying it for her. And she was actually reliving that experience now on the table in the sense that she was able to describe the smells, hear the sounds, and see the events as clearly as if she were really there in person.

As he (she) rounded the pylon at one end of the race course, he saw he was swiftly coming up on the chariot of his friend, and he planned to sideswipe his friend, cause him to crash, and then he could go on to win the race. As we examined this, Jane came to understand that his Faulty Thought was "I can control others to get what I want." But as he rammed his own chariot into that of his friend, his own wheel cracked instead, and he was thrown from his chariot, which then fell on top of him, crushing his chest. The chariot was, of course, the large heavy box which Jane had felt crushing her chest. Also, as the chariot fell, a large metal screw was loosened and was rammed into his neck and tore it open. As he lay dying under his chariot, his last thoughts were, "I'm better than this! This isn't supposed to be happening!" I then asked Jane what she would like to do next about this scene, and she immediately said, "I need to change what happened." So I took her back into the race just before he ran into his friend, and asked her how she would now like to change the events. She responded, "Don't run into my friend!" So I then had her watch as they both raced side by side toward the finish line. However, neither he nor his friend won the race, so sideswiping his friend would have been in vain anyway.

After the race, I asked the young man and his friend to embrace in friendship as gallant competitors and go to the local tavern to celebrate with a little ale. While they were laughing and talking with each other, I was intuitively guided to ask the young man to look deep into the eyes of his friend, and I asked Jane if she recognized the friend. She shouted, "Oh, my God! It's my son!" The next day Jane called to say that there had been a remarkable turnaround in the attitude of her son toward her, and that he had actually sat down with her and discussed how he felt about himself with her! When the negative patterns in her energy field were removed, the way that her energy field interacted with that of her son's energy field had changed significantly!

Case 3: Inspired Guidance Whether one believes in past lives or not does not alter the reality presented from the client's subconscious mind. If I truly believe that the sky is green, that does not alter the fact that it appears blue to everyone else. While there may be several different interpretations of what is observed, there is usually one or more underlying universal Truths with a capital "T" that cannot be denied. Many times these universal truths come through on the Ro-Hun table. One such universal Truth is "Do unto others what you would have them do unto you." The Golden Rule, the Universal Law of Cause and Effect, the concept of Karma.

Let me illustrate how this Universal Law works with another example. During the third of four Ro-Hun sessions, I was stirring up the energies in the emotional layer of Sally's Heart Chakra, and she began to see a sailboat on a lake. When we zoomed in to see who was on the sailboat, Sally began to describe two people: one was a small Asian woman, whom she knew to be herself, and the other was a hideous, mean, and loathsome bald man wearing a blue shirt.

I asked Sally to describe what each of them was doing, and she said that the ugly, hateful man was tying a rope very securely to the end of the boom to which the sail was attached. Then he wrapped the other end of the rope around her neck, and she was not strong enough to prevent it. Then he said, "It will look just like an accident. The next time the boom swings out, it will choke her and drag her overboard." He said it with a lot of malice because he hated her and Asians in general. To him, it would be just like killing a rat. He thought, "There's too many rats, and they must all be killed."

The woman screamed in terror, and knew he was completely crazy, but was not strong enough to prevent what she knew was going to happen. Then all of a sudden, the boom swung out as the wind shifted, and it hit her in the head, mouth, and shoulder. As Sally watched the scene unfold, I suggested that she would feel no pain, and that she could continue to describe what happened. Sally said that there was "a lot of red goo" coming out of her throat and shoulder area, and then she was carried out over the water and then slammed back into the side of the boat, breaking her neck. The Asian woman then died hanging tangled in the rope.

On the table, Sally was visibly upset and sobbed and I calmed her quickly with a few positive suggestions. I then asked Sally to take her awareness back into that Asian woman and describe what was happening as she died. She described going into a "spiritual place" where everything was light and bright. When I asked how she felt there, Sally replied that she felt "ecstatic," beyond joy and happiness. She said, "I feel just great! The payback went perfectly!"

Well, that was the last thing that I—as a therapist—had expected her to say, and I felt we both needed to understand more of what had really happened at the end of that lifetime. So I guided Sally's awareness back to the Asian woman, had her look into the eyes of the loathsome man, and then follow the energy of that hate in his eyes back, back, back to its source. Very soon, Sally began to describe a primitive farming community where all the townspeople were gathered around at some sort of meeting. When we looked closer, Sally described a trial being held out in the open with a judge pronouncing sentence for all offenses that came before him. Sally knew that she was that judge, and saw herself looking out on the accused from a sort of raised dias.

The next person to come before him (her) was a small Asian woman who had been accused of stealing some sweet potatoes. With no defense, the woman was found guilty, and the judge sentenced her to be tied by the hands behind a cart and dragged in the dirt until she died. Everyone thought that the sentence was unusually harsh, but no one dared oppose the judge, so the sentence was carried out. The judge felt no remorse or compassion, and he did not care that the punishment was out of proportion to the crime.

When I asked what the connection was between these two lifetimes she had witnessed, Sally replied that in the earlier lifetime she had been the judge and had unnecessarily caused the death of the Asian woman accused of stealing sweet potatoes. Therefore, she (the judge) must also experience a brutal death as an Asian woman to fully understand, on a soul level, both sides of what she had caused as the judge. The second lifetime as the Asian woman on the ship was that "payback" experience!

Also of interest was Sally's great joy at seeing that "the payback went perfectly." Sally expressed great relief and happiness that the slate was now clear. I then asked Sally to obtain the meaning of these two lifetimes from her Higher Self, and she replied, "The Law of Cause and Effect is eternal. Speak from your heart, not your mind!" After the session was over, Sally admitted that, although the karmic slate was clear with respect to these two specific previous experiences, she had recently been considering taking action against one of her coworkers which, under this broader perspective of the Law of Cause and Effect, probably would have required a future karmic payback. In this case, Sally had been given a great gift—a gentle reminder that she should not create a situation that would require a future "payback." And yet the choice of what course of action she should take was still left to her, so her own free will had not been restricted.

Advanced Processes

When Ro-Hun clients finish the Purification Series, one or more Skim Sessions, and the "Shadow Self" Series, there are several additional advanced processes available for further enlightenment. These complete the emotional release and transformation sequence in a manner that gives the client an enlightened view of Self as a spiritual being, and also permits himself to be placed in proper perspective as a cosmic being and citizen of this universe. These include the Inner Child Healing Series, the Origin Process, the Seven Visions Process, the Divine Mother Process, and the Male/Female Analysis Process.

Inner Child Healing Series This process heals and releases the mental "constructs" we create to get through intolerable situations; the "vaults" or "rooms" where we keep our four primary fears (abandonment, failure, nothingness, and death); and the "tanks" in our lower three chakras where mortally damaging emotions of abuse, deception, hatred/rage, and death wishes can be found.

When we experience trauma in our lives, we create what we need to feel better or avoid the pain of the traumatic situation. For example, if a child is in an abusive situation, she will create whatever she needs to survive. It may be an alternate personality or behavior which she believes may be acceptable to the abusive parent, or it may be an imaginary theater room or costume department that has all the different masks and makeup she believes she needs to survive. Alternatively, if the child is not allowed to express anger, she may then create a safe space in her mind she can enter to flail and scream. If she needs to take that anger out on Mom and Dad, the child might even find them in that room tied to a tree and the child is poking them with pins. These are, of course, all imaginary escape mechanisms or mental constructs used by the child to deal with an intolerable set of reality circumstances. Usually, only a few mental constructs are created. Examples might include the Chameleon who becomes what others want her to be, the Punisher who wants to get back at someone (or Self) for some wrongdoing, or Pollyannas who create a loving, nurturing place for themselves because they do not have any love in the real world.

This session deals with identifying the mental constructs and the real-life situations that send a person into these constructs, and how they affect the person's daily life. Then the inner child who created these constructs is located and comforted. The child created these constructs, and the child is the only one who can dismantle them. After all constructs are dismantled and the inner child is empowered, the inner child is then taken to the Garden of the One Who Cares (the Higher Self) until the next session. All of the energy work is done in the Brow Chakra during this session.

The second session deals with the vaults (fears) that the child would have dropped into if they went into each mental construct. Here the energy work is done in the Heart Chakra. Four primary fears have been identified, with all other fears coming under one or more of these: fear of abandonment, fear of failure, fear of nothingness, and fear of death. Each of these fears is portrayed during the session as a room into which you must enter. The client must name it and claim it as their own, and with the help and guidance of the therapist, release that fear by completely understanding how that fear was created and what effect it has on their daily life. Only then will the room be destroyed by the client's inner child. The room and the fear are an illusion, a *maya*, that was created by their own inner child, and only their own inner child can eliminate it. After all rooms are eliminated, the inner child is again taken to the Garden of the One Who Cares. After the session, the therapist and client will match up which mental construct leads to which vault. Invariably, there is a clear one-to-one matching pattern presented.

The third and fourth sessions deal with the emotional "tanks" found in the lower three chakras which correspond to the mental constructs and vaults discovered in the first two sessions. The tanks are the tanks of Abuse, Deception, Hatred/Rage, and Death Wishes. Each tank has an inner and outer chamber representing the other-directed and self-directed aspects of each damaging emotion. For example, the outer chamber of the Deception Tank represents how I deceive others and how they deceive me; the inner chamber represents how I deceive myself. Each chamber of each tank must be entered, owned, understood, and ultimately destroyed by the client's inner child.

Of particular attention is the inner chamber of the Death Wishes tank. When we get into a situation that is really intolerable (e.g., a failing marriage, never taking the time to nourish self, an abusive relationship at work, etc.) and we do nothing about it, we may begin to think, "I wish I were dead!" or "I can't live like this!" If that thought persists, it becomes a belief, and the body may soon obey by developing a life-threatening disease, such as cancer. Each Death Wish thought that the client has ever held is dealt with. As each inner and outer tank for each Death Wish thought is entered, understood, and destroyed, the client's inner child is healed, and the client is strongly empowered to take back control of their life and to restore the will to live a positive, fulfilling, and happy life.

At the end of the fourth session, the therapist and client match up each tank to each mental construct and vault. This discussion serves to crystallize in the conscious mind all the discoveries they have made about themselves during these four sessions, particularly in how their own beliefs and thoughts have been influencing or affecting their life.

Origin Process   Origin Process is designed to understand how archetypal energies affect your daily life. In the spiritual realm, the Divine Male (Father of Manifestation) and the Divine Female (Mother of Life) come together as a single energy and create a Divine Child (Mission or Purpose) for the purpose of expressing themselves in the physical world. The Divine Child is expressed as the male or female energies in the earth plane. This allows it to acquire additional experience and information, particularly regarding dealings and relationships with others. How that Divine Child expresses itself is chosen through its occupation, interests, and interactions set up for the lifetime before incarnation.

We have seen earlier that the beliefs and emotional patterns taken on *in utero* by the developing fetus are very strongly influenced by the mental and emotional energy fields of the mother. The reactive patterns of the Divine Child are similarly determined by the intentions and beliefs of the Divine Male and Divine Female archetypal energies. As the Divine Child archetypal energy becomes associated with an individual's soul expression, God's light, love, and energy are often perceived as not being fully present—the soul expression adopts a feeling of *separation* from its Source. This feeling of separateness may leave the client in a state of suffering, terror, rage, hopelessness, or guilt at being "abandoned" by God. This is the drama so often referred to as the "Garden of Eden Experience."

In the Origin Process, the Ro-Hun therapist guides the client from the Garden of Eden into the world and feelings of separateness from their Source, and assists them to remember their Source. In this way, the separation feelings and the reactions to these feelings are healed, and the Divine Child within the client can forgive and release these erroneous beliefs and feelings, and one can then return the Divine Father, Divine Mother, and Divine Child energies to the Source and satisfactorily reconcile the separation experience.

During the second session of the Origin Process (clearing the ego), additional energy work is done to determine where any patterns of abandonment may be stored in the client's energy field, and to release that energy. Each chakra is scanned with the hand, and when an issue of abandonment is found, the client is regressed to the point in time when they felt separated or abandoned. These experiences are then healed and released.

Many experiences of abandonment may be found in the lower six chakras; each is systematically investigated and released. At the conclusion of the session, the client is guided into a Sanctuary experience where he may listen to the wisdom of his guides and remain in the comforting healing energies for awhile.

Seven Visions Process   This is a three-session series that cleanses and purifies all the energies in each chakra on a very deep level. Beginning with the Heart Chakra, the client gets in touch with the One Who Cares, the Christ-Consciousness energy. This pure unconditionally loving energy is then used to cleanse the Heart Chakra and each of the lower and upper three chakras. A guided imagery process is used to introduce and heal the primary personality present in each chakra: Root Chakra—Presence; Sacral Chakra—The Emotional One; Solar Plexus Chakra—The Achiever; Throat Chakra—The Expressor; Brow Chakra—The Visionary; and Crown Chakra—The Angel.

The Heart, Root, Sacral and Solar Plexus Chakras are visited and cleansed during the first session, the Throat Chakra is addressed during the second session, and the Brow and Crown Chakras are addressed during the third session. As in the Purification Series, past-life experiences may be encountered in any of the chakras during the cleansing and healing process.

Divine Mother Process This process deals with your relationship to your mother and any negative effects this relationship has on your daily life. If after the "Shadow Self" Series there are still significant mother issues remaining, they can be resolved here. An example of a contract you may have made as a child with your mother is that you would always be quiet and obedient and never tell your mother your problems, and she would not scold you for having to take time from her hectic day to deal with your feelings and problems. In this kind of a contract, you both get something positive out of it, but there is also a negative energy sent and received by both sides.

This negative energy is felt by the therapist as a cord of energy between a specific chakra of the client and the client's mother. This energy cord binds them together until the contract is broken by both client and mother; the energy of the contract (the cord felt by the therapist) then dissolves and is released. Contracts made during the womb experience are found in the first and second chakras, and contracts made when the client was five years old are found in the Solar Plexus Chakra. Contracts of the ten-year-old are found in the Heart Chakra, the fifteen-year-old's are in the Throat Chakra, and the twenty-one-year-old's contracts are in the Brow Chakra.

After all the energetic cords are cut in each chakra, the client is then guided to find the Divine Mother and examine all the aspects of the

Divine Mother that appear fearful. She may be overpowering, controlling, or manipulative. Once these aspects of the Divine Mother have been healed and released, any unhealthy contracts that the client may have made with Mother Earth are healed and released. The client is then free to claim his space on the earth and stand in his own power to fulfill his true purpose on earth.

Male/Female Analysis Process This process addresses potential imbalances in the male and female energies within the client. As a rough rule of thumb, each woman's energies are about two-thirds female and one-third male, and each man's energies are about two-thirds male and one-third female. When these energies become significantly unbalanced in one direction or the other, the people and situations we attract usually contribute to an unbalanced relationship with others. However, when the desired balance of male and female energies is shown by both partners, relationships are healed and transformed since there is love, value, and respect not only for your partner, but also for your own inner male and female selves.

Here, the client learns that he or she must reach out to the opposite side of their own personality (male for women, female for men) and be comfortable with the fact that he or she really does need the opposite aspect to be complete and whole. Metaphorically, each sex needs to see the other as the opposite side of the same coin, and not as separate coins.

Up to three sessions are required for the Male/Female Analysis Process due to the time required to deal with several levels of issues in each of the chakras. The guided imagery begins, as all Ro-Hun processes do, in a relaxed state. Here, the client sees the male and female aspects of themselves, and begins to describe what each is doing. If the female is lying in the bed waiting and the male is sitting reading the paper, some major work is needed to bring these aspects into balance! Each aspect is worked with and healed until a relationship develops where each is nourished by the energy of the other. Then and only then can the client begin to recognize and fulfill their purpose in life, drawing on the complementary energies of each aspect, rather than living in a continual battle where one aspect demands domination of the other.

Three levels of male/female analysis are conducted in each chakra, and each level may involve a different issue, situation, or circumstance in which one aspect of a personality dominates the other. The types of issues and situations generally correspond to the chakra being worked at that time. For example, in the Solar Plexus Chakra, a woman's female part may believe that oneness can never be felt, so the male aspect dominates and tries to be an overachiever to compensate. The woman may then appear to others as very competitive, aggressive, and dominating. She must be shown how to heal the wounded female aspect within so that it can express equally in her dealings with others. This immediately results in the emergence of her soft, warm, loving nature, thus enabling her to attract this in others.

Summary

If you are happy with your life the way it is, do *not* try Ro-Hun. Ro-Hun will positively transform the way you think about yourself and about others! However, Ro-Hun is not for everyone; you must be willing and prepared to deal with the unpleasant and dark issues of your psyche. But if you are ready to confront and let go of your fears, phobias, negative thoughts, and belief systems, Ro-Hun will transform your life and give you a more positive and confident, yet compassionate and understanding view of yourself. This positive "new you" will be projected outward as your newly repatterned energy field interacts with the energy fields of others, and you will attract positive people, experiences, and opportunities to you.

The Ro-Hun process will probably be emotionally intense for most people. The great majority of my Ro-Hun clients react deeply to the scenes and feelings they bring up, and tissues are always kept at hand. However, as each issue is worked through, there is such a feeling of release felt by the client that he is always encouraged to continue the process with the next chakra until each is energetically cleaned, balanced, and renewed. Since several chakras may be dealt with in a single Table Session, many emotional issues can also be released during that session. In addition to the emotional releases experienced by the client, he is also provided a significantly broader insight into his energetic, emotional, mental, and spiritual makeup through Ro-Hun than is available through more traditional therapies.

With the release of her negative energies, the client is free to attract the positive experiences of life, to learn to open her heart and love unconditionally with compassion and understanding for others. In this process, she also continues to grow and evolve as she becomes aware of and incorporates a much broader and higher perspective of her daily activities. As each of us becomes more aware of what we are as cosmic, spiritual beings, we also become more capable of creating happiness, fulfillment, and joy in our lives and in the lives of those around us.

Ro-Hun is an inspired process of personal growth and transformation founded by Patricia Hayes in 1983. Hayes is the cofounder and the Chairperson of the Board of Directors of Delphi University in McCaysville, Georgia, and is also the Director of the Ro-Hun Institute at Delphi. Formal training in all basic and advanced Ro-Hun processes is conducted regularly at the Ro-Hun Institute at the baccalaureate, master's, and doctorate levels. In addition, formal training in Ro-Hun processes at the baccalaureate level (Cleanse, Skim, Purification Series, and the "Shadow Self" Series) is conducted periodically at the Graham Institute of Self-Awareness (GISA) in Yorktown, Virginia. For further information, see Appendix C, page 144.

Awakening the
Spiritual Energy Body

The root or base chakra is the storehouse for a natural, yet powerful, energy called the kundalini. This kundalini energy has the
potential to activate and align all of the major chakras with the
higher centers, bringing illumination and spiritual enlightenment
with the proper sequence of chakra unfoldment.

—Dr. Richard Gerber, *Vibrational Medicine*

In chapters 2 through 4 we intro-
duced the four densest energy bodies in the Human Energy Field
(physical, etheric, emotional, and mental), and discussed various healing techniques and modalities that repattern the energetic vibrations
of these bodies for greater harmony and health on those levels. The
outer energy body of the Human Energy Field is the Spiritual Body.
This body contains the vibrational patterns associated with the awareness of our true, spiritual nature. It also holds the patterns of the
lessons we have agreed to learn during the current life expression, both
in relation to our own personal growth and evolution, and also having
to do with our relationship with others—our karmic intentions
involved in situations allowing us to work out previous karmic debts.

Therefore, it is "perfect" in and of itself, and does not need to be
repatterned for greater health. However, in most individuals, awareness

of our spiritual nature and the Spiritual Body lies dormant and does not affect our conscious life to a significant degree. For this to happen, we simply need to "remember" who and what we are, and why we are here doing what we are doing. When this happens and we are consciously aware of the patterns in our Spiritual Body, we become enlightened beings and are truly aware of our unique and vital role in the drama of the cosmos.

Thaddeus Golas, in his book *The Lazy Man's Guide to Enlightenment*, writes: "Enlightenment is any experience of expanding our consciousness beyond its present limits. Perfect enlightenment is realizing that we have no limits at all—and that the entire universe is alive."[1] All is energy, not only in this dimension, but also in all higher dimensions and planes of existence. When we choose to attune to this truth, we have begun to claim our true place as a cosmic citizen in a living universe.

Activation of the Spiritual Body can be accomplished by energizing the internal energies inherent in each of us—the kundalini energy associated with the Root Chakra. This is normally done by one's self as the result of long-term introspection, meditation, and other techniques originally associated with the yogic path to mystic illumination.

Many books have been written on how to meditate and on the benefits of meditation. But they all come down to the same thing: it is a practice you have to master yourself and no one can help you other than on points of technique. Meditation is a personal experience, and as such, each person learns from repeated experience whether or not certain postures, mantras, or music are appropriate to aid them in entering a meditative state.

There is growing evidence that repeated meditation *does* have a discernable physiological effect on the brain and on the body. Electrical brain wave activity generated by the two hemispheres of the brain are more in step and function with greater coherence in meditators than in non-meditators.[2] Long-term meditators also frequently gain the ability to consciously control certain physiological body functions such as heart rate, blood pressure, and skin temperature.[3]

During the meditation process, various techniques are used to focus the attention inward to experience the awareness of the present moment. These techniques include listening to your own heartbeat, becoming aware of your breath as it enters and leaves your body, or expanding your awareness to include and recognize all aspects of what it means to be "alive" in your version of reality. Over a period of time, this introspection and meditation begins to develop the nervous system in such a way allowing deeper levels of consciousness, and encouraging the release and flow of energy within one's own internal energy system.

Kundalini meditation—that is, meditation with the intent of raising one's kundalini energies for the ultimate purpose of spiritual enlighten-ment—"offers a clear, experience-based approach for awakening our mundane minds to the presence of our true spiritual nature."4 When one learns to still the mind chatter that normally frustrates the begin-ning meditator, we can experience the flow of life force through our body, allow our consciousness to rise and expand to new levels, and exist in the infinite moment of the present. But until recently, you your-self have had to learn how to allow the kundalini to rise within you to achieve the ultimate state of bliss that is said to be associated with spir-itual enlightenment.

Now there is a remarkable new technique called Light Energization that allows a trained practitioner to accelerate the rise of kundalini and the awakening of the Spiritual Body of another person. However, before we discuss this technique, I would be negligent if I did not emphasize that awakening your own kundalini is not without its perils if you are not fully prepared for the experience. To offer this technique to another who is not fully prepared is totally irresponsible, and can be karmically disastrous for the practitioner. For this reason, we need to discuss what kundalini energy *is,* how it affects the human energy bodies, and how to energetically prepare one's self for the kundalini experience.

Kundalini Energy

In yogic and Hindu literature, kundalini is the process that activates the energy of the chakras, and also assists in awakening the higher centers of consciousness. In many ancient texts, the kundalini energy is depicted as a coiled snake that normally lies sleeping in the Root Chakra. When this energy is unleashed through a deliberate process such as meditation, it rises up the central energy column just in front of the spine, activating each chakra along the way. When kundalini energy reaches the third eye and Crown Chakra, the individual may experience a sensation of bright light flooding the brain, followed by expansion of the consciousness, and a feeling of intense bliss.

This can be a beautiful, overwhelming experience of pure ecstasy which, if repeated regularly, can lead to spiritual enlightenment. But if the subject is not fully prepared, it can also be an extremely painful and damaging experience resulting in severe physical, emotional, and mental scars. The kundalini energy is very strong, and if it encounters any blocks in the chakras as it rises toward the crown, negative side effects are quite possible.

Richard Gerber describes the chakras as "the energy repositories of karma."[5] If complete chakra cleansing is not accomplished *before* attempting to raise the kundalini, these patterns constrict and distort the free rising flow of kundalini energy as it reaches the chakras. The kundalini energy will continue to hammer away at these energy blocks until they are burned through. As we have seen in previous chapters, there are several techniques and processes to repattern the physical and etheric energy bodies, and the Ro-Hun technique has been expressly developed to remove negative or nonharmonious energy patterns from the emotional and mental levels of each chakra.

Kundalini energy has been compared to an electrical current that passes through the thin filament of a lightbulb. As the current passes through, light and burning heat may be produced. The more resistance to the current, the more heat and light are produced. Blockages in the chakras to the flow of kundalini energy must be removed before the flow of energy will be smooth.

All this is said not with the intent to discourage the kundalini experience; instead it is intended to encourage proper preparation before attempting to raise your kundalini energy yourself, or request that a trained practitioner assist you in this process. The key is the preparation of all chakras by clearing the negative energies from each, and balancing the energies between and among the chakras. When this has been done, the kundalini has a clear and free energetic pathway to travel.

As a matter of course, I insist that my clients satisfactorily complete at least the basic Ro-Hun Purification and "Shadow Self" Series prior to beginning any Light Energization sessions. This allows me to monitor the energetic clearing progress in each of their chakras. It also provides the client with enough information to decide when he feels he is ready to proceed with the Light Energization process.

I offer Light Energization sessions as an adjunct to the client's own meditation program. At the point where Light Energization sessions are appropriate for a client, he will already be well on his way up his own spiritual mountain, and will have found meditation techniques and practices appropriate for himself. In addition, he will recognize his own path to walk, and know that no one can walk it for him. The Light Energization sessions are offered as a means of assisting the client in accelerating the beneficial effects of their own regular meditation. It is not a technique where some practitioner can magically cause another person to become enlightened. It just does not work that way.

The number of Light Energization sessions that a client may feel is appropriate will be determined at least in part by his own level of spiritual awareness. If he has been meditating regularly for years and has experienced beneficial kundalini releases during meditation, perhaps only one or two sessions will be required to balance the male and female aspects of the kundalini energy (ida and pingala) as it flows upward through the chakras. Alternatively, for one who is meditating regularly but has not experienced a kundalini release, several sessions may be required to encourage the gentle release and controlled kundalini flow. And as in all other forms of energy-based healing, the client's Higher Self is always in charge of accepting or rejecting the energies offered by the healing practitioner.

Light Energization

This technique was developed by Mauricio Panisset, a modest and very compassionate Brazilian healer who was also known as "The Man of Lights." During his healing sessions, flashes of light similar to a flashbulb going off would be spontaneously emitted from his hands. Shirley MacLaine devotes a chapter to Mr. Panisset and his phenomenal healing work in her book, *Going Within*.[6]

Light Energization helps bring into the client's awareness the conscious realization and knowledge that her true nature is that of a spiritual being undergoing a human physical experience (a lifetime). The Light Energization practitioner assists in the process of gently and safely opening the kundalini energy pathways within the client. This allows the client to, in her own time and at her own pace, raise her consciousness to higher planes for further enlightenment.

The following general description of a Light Energization session is given to provide a basic understanding of what to expect during the session, and also to illustrate the intricacy and depth of training required to conduct such a session. However, the process is purposely not described in the detail necessary to actually conduct a Light Energization session. A very thorough understanding of the client's energetic nature and state of chakra health is required on the part of the therapist. In addition, much of the effectiveness of this technique is determined by the energy and power of the healer's spoken word to direct the flow of energy within the client. Since this technique was developed in Brazil, many of the key phrases that direct the process of awakening the client's kundalini energy are spoken in Portuguese as well as in English.

Preparation Prior to an Energization session, it is important that the healing space, the client, and the healer all be specifically and separately prepared. A healing table, usually a massage table, is used to provide comfortable support to the client's body during a Light Energization session. The healing energies present during the session are of a very high vibrational nature, and occasionally the client may slip into an altered state. Therefore, the client should be lying down and not in a chair. Other room preparations include the use of rose-scented candles, and a specially chosen version of "Ave Maria" playing continuously at a moderate level in the healing room. Rather than having it play softly in the background, the louder volume and continuous repetition becomes a musical mantra that in itself invokes very high spiritual vibrations.

The client will be asked to attend the Light Energization session dressed entirely in white clothing, preferably cotton. The healer will be similarly dressed. This provides a subliminal cue regarding the purity of intention of both healer and client for the session. (This is also why most doctors' smocks are white.) After being placed on the table, the client is allowed to relax for a few moments into the aural and olfactory cues (music and rose essence) provided.

While the client is becoming relaxed, the healer will begin to focus his or her attention and intention on the sacredness of the work to be done during the session. Through specific breathing exercises, the healer begins to lift his consciousness and expand his auric field to encompass the client with unconditional love and compassion.

Join Energy Fields When an energetic connection is established on the higher levels of the auric field, the healer will then make physical contact with the client's body, usually near the Brow Chakra, to ensure that the healer's field and the client's energy fields are fully connected on all levels. By working around the head near the Brow Chakra, the healer is able to relax the client even further and smooth out the vibrational patterns, particularly on the mental level. By energetically removing stagnant or negative patterns in the mental body, the client is relaxed even further.

Balance Brain Energies Continuing to work around the head area, the healer will use specific movements to balance the right-left, male-female energies between the two hemispheres of the brain. A combination of a specific breathing techniques, intention, and hand movements is then used to begin activating the client's energy column from the Root Chakra up through the Crown Chakra (pineal gland).

Awaken Kundalini in Lower Chakras Continuing to work physically around the head area near the brow and Crown Chakras, the healer uses the breath and inner senses to gently stimulate and awaken the kundalini energies in the Root Chakra. The male-female, left-right, ida-pingala aspects of the kundalini energy are then again balanced and energized at a level which is safe for the client's prior chakra cleansing and preparation work. Once energetically stimulated and energized, the kundalini is then gently brought up through the client's energy system, one chakra at a time through the first, second, and third chakras.

Connect to Heart Chakra As the healer makes a physical connection between the brow and Heart Chakras of the client, a specific breathwork process is begun to open the Heart Chakra and bring the kundalini energy up gently into it. As this gateway for the higher energetic forces is opened and activated, loving assistance is called upon from the higher planes to acknowledge and accept the kundalini energies from the lower chakras (representing the energies of the physical body) and transform these energies through unconditional love into their highest aspects. It is at this point that the beauty and energy of the Portuguese language is brought into full expression, and then followed with the English translation so that the full impact and beauty of the kundalini transformation can be experienced with very deep feelings and emotions.

Awaken Kundalini in Upper Chakras This transformed kundalini energy is then brought up into the Throat, Brow, and Crown Chakras as the client is encouraged to open himself into new dimensions of expression, vision, sensitivity, and awareness. Again, specific breathing motions and sounds are made to facilitate the rising movement of the kundalini energy.

Heal and Balance Entire Energy System Working around the head area first, the ida-pingala aspects of the kundalini energies are again balanced in the Brow and Crown Chakras, and within the general head and shoulders area. The client's entire energetic envelope is then balanced, proceeding from head and shoulders, down the trunk to the hips, and down each leg to the ankles, and finally, the energy of love is blown down into the aura of his feet.

Energize the Crown Chakra When the energy system is fully balanced, the healer returns to the head area and connects the Brow Chakra and one shoulder while energizing the Crown Chakra with a specific breathing technique.

Close the Crown Chakra Moving the hands in a particular circular motion through the Crown Chakra, the client is reminded that he is a part of God, and God is a part of him. Peace, clarity, tranquility, and special protection are invoked for the client, after which he is allowed to rest for a few minutes in the very high vibrational energies present.

Ground and Release the Client When the client is ready, he is gently grounded as in any healing session, and then gently raised to a sitting position on the table until he is clear-headed and able to walk steadily. A glass of water is always offered after every healing session to help the grounding process. Following the session, I always ask for impressions received during the session, and for general feedback about how the session was perceived. This additional time also allows the client to return fully to a waking state before driving or going home.

For further information on the Light Energization process, see Appendix C, page 144.

Growing Home

Verily, verily, I say unto you, He that believeth on me, the works that
I do shall he do also; and greater works than these shall he do. . . .

—The Master Jesus (John 14:12)

In the preceding chapters we have discussed several healing techniques that can be used on others to promote the healing of specific energy bodies, including the physical body. However, these represent only a fraction of the energy-based healing techniques currently available when planning a holistic program for returning to—and maintaining—a state of complete health. As mentioned in the preface, these techniques are only those to which I have been drawn. You may also be drawn to these too, or possibly to others.

It is also important to note that each technique operates primarily on the level discussed, but through the principle of sympathetic vibration, the adjacent energy bodies may also be simultaneously addressed. For example, Reiki works primarily on the physical body, but with our broader perspective of how energy healing works, we have learned that much of the healing work is done on the etheric body, the pattern for the physical. Through resonance of vibrations into the higher octaves, the higher emotional and mental bodies can also be affected in a positive manner.

Through this broader understanding of how healing works, we can more clearly appreciate that the human body is only the densest level of manifestation of our true multilevel energetic nature. Just the mere fact that each of us has an energy field surrounding our physical body should stimulate a curiosity to understand what that field *represents,* and what *happens* when *my* field comes into contact with *your* field. We need to understand what we truly are and how we interact energetically with others. This understanding will give us the knowledge to begin exploring the real meaning of health and disease on several levels.

The Healer Within You

As some slowly begin to search for how best to apply this new knowledge for their own health or the health of others, they awaken to the first sparks of the real meaning of life itself. However, not all individuals are willing to take those baby steps just now; they are willing to be content in the valley and will still wonder what the view from the mountaintop is like. But those who take their journey upward begin to see the real importance of the journey itself. Each time they reach a higher vantage point, they are able to see their entire journey from an even higher perspective.

A reasonable question to ask at this point is, "Now that I have this broader understanding, this greater perspective, this additional knowledge of healing techniques, how can I apply it in my own daily life?" The interesting thing is that it can be applied any way you want to use it in your daily life. You could choose to become a healer, but you do not necessarily have to. You could be a waitress, a chief financial officer, a policeman, a teacher, an engineer, or whatever, and still find very practical use for this new knowledge in your daily interactions with others.

Each step up the stairs of understanding will surely change how you view yourself, how you view others, how you interact with others, and how you view and participate in your own reality. Each new belief you adopt for yourself, about others, and about your own reality, will change the vibrational patterns in your mental body—either in a positive or negative fashion.

These new beliefs and vibrational patterns in your mental body, about your "universe," will automatically generate some response becoming a new pattern in your emotional body. You may feel relieved, refreshed, wonder, awe, and joy; alternatively, you may feel confused, depressed, worthless, insignificant, or lonely. You have your free will choice, and can choose either response. That response, however, will become a new part of your emotional body—how you "feel" about yourself and others. This in turn will affect the etheric body, the pattern for the physical body.

Let us return to the question of how to make practical, day-to-day use of this additional knowledge of who and what we are. Perhaps you would like your path to be similar to mine, that of a healer. First, ask yourself if it "feels right." If not, use the new information in your own line of work to recognize that each person you meet, every man, woman, and child that enters your life, is on their own chosen path and at the correct place in that path for them at that time. Use this insight with compassion, and accept that person without judgment just as they are, for they have chosen to be what and where they are on their own path, just as you have also chosen to be what and where you are on your own path. Send them unconditional love and support if they are challenged in any way. A kind word or even a seemingly insignificant but graciously offered deed such as a friendly smile or a kind word may be just what that person needs most at that time.

But if your deep desires lead you toward the path of healing as a means of helping others, you may wonder if anyone at all can become a healer, or if that is a special talent bestowed upon a chosen few. If you believe that healing is something that only a few specially chosen people can do, ask yourself: "Who is doing the choosing?"

This question has three possible answers: God, yourself, or "someone else" who has control over your desires and capabilities. In a universe where Free Will is one of the fundamental principles, the first and last possible answers just do not make sense. You yourself will make the choice to become a healer. But how good a healer you become will depend upon your sincerity, your commitment, and upon your previous experience and knowledge as a healer.

If you have absolutely no knowledge of healing and have never been a healer before, the vibrational patterns in your higher energy bodies that would subconsciously draw you toward healing may be absent altogether. But very few of us have never had an experience of healing someone else on some level, or have never experienced a healing act from someone else. Even the gentle reassurance to a child that her skinned knee "will soon be better" is healing on many levels.

Each time we participate in a healing experience, either as healer or client, our beliefs and feelings are affected one way or another. Repeated positive experiences create permanent vibrational patterns in our higher energy bodies, and these vibrational energy patterns are carried forward from one life experience to the next. Those who are strongly drawn to become healers are probably simply remembering their previously gained knowledge and abilities.

Anyone can learn to become a healer if they choose to and feel strongly enough that healing is their path, just as anyone can learn to play the piano or paint a fine picture if that is how she wants to express her own individuality to herself and to others. If the healing path is chosen and you set out to assist others in their own return to health, the knowledge you gain about healing along the way will automatically give you new vistas of what and who you are as a person.

Your identity as an individual, that of a separate being who interacts with others, is defined not by your name or your height or the color of your eyes, but by what you do with the abilities that you have right now, and by the motives involved in your actions and deeds. As you learn how to assist in the healing of others, you will soon realize that you are healing yourself, too. Just the knowledge (as opposed to the belief) that you can actually assist others to accelerate their own healing is a quantum step forward in the perception of who you are as a person and as a spiritual being, and of what you are truly capable. The actual experience of being a healer allows us to grow beyond what we previously believed were our limitations. In fact, we begin to awaken to the fact that our only limitations are the ones that we create for ourselves individually by faulty or shortsighted belief systems or thought patterns.

Awakening to a New Reality

As each of us goes through our daily routine, we interact with our environment and with others in accordance with our beliefs and perceptions, our likes and dislikes, our biases and prejudices, and our emotions and feelings. Whatever vibrational patterns we have stored in our energy field are radiated out to and are felt by others, even if on a subliminal level. And our interpretation of how others react to us becomes a part of our field also.

If others do not feel comfortable with you and your actions, they will shy away; if this pattern continues, you may come to question your own worth or value as a person. "Why don't people like me?" might turn into "Why am I always rejected?" and this might eventually become "I am unworthy to have friends." But if you are radiating warmth, friendliness, compassion, and tolerance from your energy field, people will subconsciously respond with a similar reaction and be drawn to you.

In this way we actually create our own reality—our own perception of the world we live in. But when we consciously recognize the fact that we have the ability to create what is desirable in our life, we empower ourselves to such a degree that our life is truly changed forever. All we have to do is choose to live with unconditional love and compassion for others and set aside forever the anger, fear, jealousy, hate, greed, and any other negative reaction that we may have had in our energy field.

The new reality that each of us can create for ourselves is limited only by what we can imagine is possible. And this includes a new reality of how we define and measure our own health. When the definition of health is expanded to include the vibrational patterns of each of our energy bodies, and the interrelationship of each energy body with others, we begin to see how we can start taking charge of our own health. We can begin to assume this responsibility ourselves with the understanding and knowledge of how and why disease occurs, and how health is restored.

It is time to take a good, hard, and very critical look at both allopathic and alternative medical techniques. The best of both approaches should be incorporated into an integrated healing program tailored to meet the specific needs of the client/patient on all levels of his total being. It is not enough any more to merely take three pills a day for ten days and assume you will be cured. While drugs can be very effective in combating certain kinds of infections, the potential interactions with other drugs are not fully understood in all cases. Drugs can also have a very powerful long-term effect on the body, even when only prescribed for a short while. Both these effects need to be studied in greater detail to obtain a better understanding of how and when they should be used.

Similarly, the application and effects of alternative medical therapies, and energy-based healing techniques in particular, need to be studied just as critically. The same healthy skepticism should be applied to allopathic and alternative techniques alike when attempting to determine the potential benefit of either approach to the patient/client. And should an energy-based healing technique be found in properly documented clinical trials to be effective in accelerating the client's healing, it should ideally receive the same amount of marketing hype and advertisement coverage as a new drug which has a similar effect.

Fortunately, the growing grassroots medical reform movement for inclusion of alternative medical therapies into a balanced holistic healing program is now being felt. There is a growing demand for alternative medical therapies, including energy-based healing techniques. And as traditional physicians become aware of alternative therapies and their beneficial effects, many are becoming more receptive to integrating a wide variety of alternative therapies and their normal allopathic approaches into a combined program for restoring total health. Health is coming to mean much more that just *physical* health.

As new drugs are subjected to scientifically conducted clinical trials and analysis and new surgical techniques are refined and improved, traditional medical information continues to grow rapidly. Similarly, as more becomes known about the human energy field and energy-based healing techniques, this information also needs to be seriously investigated and analyzed. However, the traditional scientific method of analysis cannot always be applied to someone's energy field to determine their state of health.

Very few people can see energy fields, and scientific instruments have not been developed yet which provide a demonstrable, repeatable, and reliable method of measuring or describing the human energy field. Instead, we have anecdotal reports, verbal descriptions, and in many cases only intuitively derived information that describes what is going on when an energy healer repatterns someone else's energy bodies. Yet this anecdotal information appears to be so consistent and repeatable, from so many different sources and healers, that the beneficial results or effects of a healing session should also be rigorously addressed.

Just because we may not understand how healing is accelerated does not invalidate the fact that it *can* be accelerated. And the acceleration can be documented quantitatively in terms of how much less pain medication is required, immune system improvements (white cell count), by how many days hospital stays are shortened, and so on. This empirically derived *synthesized information* needs to be properly documented along with the scientifically derived *analyzed information* so that the best of both approaches can be incorporated into a person's overall holistic healing program.

This is the bright new direction of the "Integrative Medicine" approach to healing, and is the basis for the medical revolution now being felt throughout all sectors of the medical community in America. Our physicians are among the best trained in the world, and that training has prepared them in the best way possible to recognize and deal with allopathic emergencies. But they can use only the tools that they have been given. In most cases, this is a knowledge of drugs and surgical skills. And these tools are simply not effective in dealing with a large number of chronic patient complaints.

However, one should not blame a physician for his lack of knowledge of helpful energy-based healing techniques. One can only practice what one has been taught. As we become aware of the significant potential for accelerating the healing process through the use of energy-based healing techniques, we will begin to seek out those doctors who are knowledgeable in this area. However, each individual doctor is also at his own chosen place, on his own path. Many traditional physicians are now beginning to investigate alternative medical therapies and are becoming more willing to collaborate with alternative medical therapists for their patient's overall best good. More and more, the traditional and alternative health practitioners will be drawn together to collaborate, to complement the other's skills, and to synergistically enhance the client's potential for returning to a healthy lifestyle of disease prevention rather than disease elimination.

I would not interfere
With any creed of yours
Or want to appear
that I have all the cures.

There is so much to know . . .
So many things are true.
The way my feet must go
May not be best for you.

And so I give this spark
Of what is Light to me,
To guide you through the dark,
But not tell you what to see.

—*Author unknown*

Appendix A:
Initial Client Interview Form

The Initial Client Interview Form shown on the following page is my own creation, and is the result of my own experience and many discussions with other alternative healing practitioners. In addition, it is a "living" form in that additional fields can be added as the need arises. A simple forms generation program ("Expert Forms for Windows" by Expert Software—about $10 at most major computer superstores) was used to generate the original form and to update it into the version you see presented here.

CONFIDENTIAL

INITIAL CLIENT INTERVIEW			

Name:		ID#	Age/DOB:	Today's Date:

Home Phone:	Work Phone:	Occupation:

Address:	Referred By:
	Childhood Religion: / Current Affiliation:

Personal Stress:	Work Stress:

Stress Reduction / Relaxation / Exercise:	Can Visualize: Yes_____ Some_____ Difficult_____ None_____
	Knows Chakras System_____ Knows Energy Bodies_____
Meditation Practice: _____Daily _____X Per Week None_____	Believes in PL_____ CM_____ CU_____ Angels_____

Current Health Care Providers:

Current Medications/Drugs (including Recreational):

Significant Past Medical History (Including Sleeping History):

Do You Smoke? ____Yes ____No

Client's Reason for Appointment:

Why Alternative Healing Instead Of Traditional Medical Treatment?

What Is Your Experience With Traditional Medical Doctors?

What Kind Of Energy-Based Healing Techniques Have You Had Before? What Were The Results? Were You Satisfied?

Would You Consider An Integrated Alternative/Traditional Approach To Healing? Why/Why Not?

Describe Your Current Lifestyle (Relationships, Home, Children, Job, Hobbies, etc.)

CONFIDENTIAL

Form INIT (8 Apr 99)

Appendix B:
Notification to Physician

(Date) _____

Dr. _____
(Address)

Dear Dr. _____,

I am a certified hypnotherapist and practitioner of energy-based alternative medical therapies, including Therapeutic Touch, Healing Touch, and Reiki. One of your patients, Ms. Jane C., has asked me to prepare a holistic healing program for her that includes weight release and which also addresses her Type I diabetes. She is now using an insulin pump, as you have prescribed.

I have advised Ms. C. that I would be willing to provide hypnotherapy sessions for weight release and energy-based healing sessions to her only on the condition that you, as her physician, are aware that she intends to incorporate these alternative healing therapies into her total healing program. Since I am not a licensed physician, I am not qualified to diagnose conditions or prescribe medications. However, I need you to be aware of her requests for weight release using hypnotherapy and for addressing her diabetes using energy-based healing techniques.

Upon your acknowledgment of the fact that Ms. C. intends to embark on this integrated approach blending both traditional allopathic and alternative medical techniques, I will begin the hypnotherapy and energy-based healing sessions with her. I estimate at this time that several healing sessions over approximately three months will be required.

I would greatly appreciate it if you would acknowledge the above information by signing and returning the statement below, and then returning this letter to me in the self-addressed stamped envelope provided, along with any considerations you feel I should be aware of.

Thank you,

Howard F. Batie
Director, Evergreen Healing Arts Center

- -

I acknowledge the above information.

_____

(Signature)

_____ _____

(Printed Name)   (Date)

Appendix C:
Resource List for Healing Modalities

Reiki

Reiki Websites

www.ozemail.com.au/~teramai/
www.reiki-seichem.com/kathleen.html
www.threshold.ca/reiki

Use the word "Reiki" in your search engine to locate other sites.

Healing Touch

Healing Touch
General Information

Colorado Center for
Healing Touch, Inc.
Attn: Cheryl Hardy
198 Union Blvd., Suite 204
Lakewood, CO 80228
e-mail: ccheal@aol.com

Healing Touch for Animals

Attn: Carol Komitor
9988 Cottoncreek Drive
Highlands Ranch, CO 80126
e-mail: htanimals@aol.com

Healing Touch
Spiritual Ministry

Attn: Linda Smith
198 Union Blvd., Suite 204
Lakewood, CO 80228
e-mail: linsmith@aol.com

Healing Touch Website

www.healingtouch.net

Reflective Healing

Delphi University
Attn: Marshall Smith
P.O. Box 70
McCaysville, GA 30555
e-mail: registrar@delphi-center.com

Ro-Hun[SM]

The Ro-Hun Institute
Attn: Patricia Hayes
P.O. Box 70
McCaysville, GA 30555
e-mail: registrar@delphi-center.com

Graham Institute of Self-Awareness
Attn: Dottie Graham
148 Breezy Point Drive
Yorktown, VA 23692
e-mail: GISAofVA@aol.com

Light Energization

The Ro-Hun Institute
Attn: Kimberley Curcio
P.O. Box 70
McCaysville, GA 30555
e-mail: registrar@delphi-center.com

Author Website

Evergreen Healing Arts Center
www.localaccess.com/HealingHands

Endnotes

Introduction

1. Ruth Montgomery, *Born to Heal* (New York: Fawcett Books Group, 1985), p. 47.

Chapter One

1. Barbara Ann Brennan, *Hands of Light* (New York: Bantam Books, 1987), p. 40.

2. Ibid., p. 41.

3. Zolar, *Dancing Heart to Heart* (McCaysville, GA: Editions Soleil, 1991), pp. 47–49.

4. For simplicity, I have aggregated all energy bodies above the Mental Body into what I call the Spiritual Body.

5. Richard Gerber, *Vibrational Medicine* (Santa Fe: Bear & Co., 1988), p. 163.

6. Brennan, *Hands of Light*, p. 49.

7. Michael Talbot, *The Holographic Universe* (New York: Harper-Perennial, 1991), p. 187.

8. Gerber, p. 115.

9. Brennan, *Hands of Light*, p. 49.

10. Ibid., pp. 148–150.

11. Ibid., p. 148.

12. Ibid., p. 149.

13. "The Healing Revolution," *Life* magazine (Sept. 1966), p. 39.

14. Louise L. Hay, *You Can Heal Your Life* (Carlsbad, CA: Hay House, Inc., 1987), pp. 146–207.

15. Gerber, p. 168.

16. Roger J. Woolger, Ph.D., *Other Lives, Other Selves* (New York: Bantam Books, 1993), pp. 167–168.

17. Barbara Ann Brennan, *Light Emerging* (New York: Bantam Books, 1993), pp. 309–310.

Chapter Two

1. Gerber, pp. 318–319.

2. "Alternate Insurance Coverage," *New Age Journal* (Fall, 1996), pp. 67–68.

3. "The Healing Revolution," *Life* magazine (Sept. 1996), p. 36.

4. Healing Touch Level I Notebook, p. 58.

Chapter Four

1. Woolger, p. 30.

2. Ibid., p. 29.

3. Ibid., pp. 254–255.

4. Michael Gabriel, *Voices from the Womb* (Lower Lake, CA: Aslan Publishing, 1992), p. 17.

5. Woolger, p. 40.

6. Ibid., p. 97.

Chapter Five

1. Thaddeus Golas, *The Lazy Man's Guide to Enlightenment* (New York: Bantam Books, 1993), p. 12.

2. Gerber, p. 402.

3. Ibid.

4. John Selby, *Kundalini Awakening* (New York: Bantam Books, 1992), p. 8.

5. Gerber, p. 400.

6. Shirley MacLaine, *Going Within* (New York: Bantam Books, 1989), p. 199 ff.

Bibliography

Ansari, Masud, Ph. D. *Modern Hypnosis: Theory and Practice* (Washington, D.C.: Mas-Press, 1991).

Bach, Richard. *Jonathan Livingston Seagull* (New York: MacMillan & Co., 1970).

Barratt, Kathleen. *Dance of Breath* (Privately Published, 1993).

Bradford, Michael. *The Healing Energy of Your Hands* (Freedom, CA: The Crossing Press, Inc., 1993).

Brennan, Barbara Ann. *Hands of Light: A Guide to Healing Through the Human Energy Field* (New York: Bantam Books, 1987).

———. *Light Emerging: The Journey of Personal Healing* (New York: Bantam Books, 1993).

Dacher, Elliott S., M.D. *Psychoneuroimmunology: The New Mind/Body Healing Program* (New York: Paragon House, 1993).

Elman, Dave. *Hypnotherapy* (Glendale, CA: Westwood Publishing Co., 1964).

Gabriel, Michael, M.A. *Voices from the Womb* (Lower Lake, CA: Aslan Publishing, 1992).

Gerber, Richard, M.D. *Vibrational Medicine: New Choices for Healing Ourselves* (Santa Fe, NM: Bear & Co., 1988).

Gindes, Bernard C., M.D. *New Concepts of Hypnosis: As an Adjunct to Psychotherapy and Medicine* (North Hollywood, CA: Wilshire Book Co., 1951).

Golas, Thaddeus. *The Lazy Man's Guide to Enlightenment* (New York: Bantam Books, 1993).

Haberly, Helen J. *Reiki: Hawayo Takata's Story* (Olney, MD: Archedigm Publications, 1990).

Hay, Louise L. *You Can Heal Your Life* (Carlsbad, CA: Hay House, Inc., 1984).

Hover-Kramer, Dorothea, Ed.D., R.N. *Healing Touch: A Resource for Health Care Professionals* (Albany, NY: Delmar Publishers, 1996).

Joy, W. Brugh, M.D. *Joy's Way: A Map for the Transformational Journey* (New York: G.P. Putnam's Sons, 1979).

Karagulla, Shafica, M.D. and Dora van Gelder Kunz. *The Chakras and the Human Energy Fields* (Wheaton, IL: Quest Books, 1989).

Kenyon, Tom, M.A. *Brain States* (Captain Cook, HI: United States Publishing, 1994).

Krasner, A. M., Ph.D. *The Wizard Within: The Krasner Method of Clinical Hypnotherapy* (Irvine, CA: American Board of Hypnotherapy Press, 1990).

MacLaine, Shirley. *Going Within: A Guide for Inner Transformation* (New York: Bantam Books, 1989).

McVoy, Cullen. *Finding Ro-Hun: Awakening Through Spiritual Therapy* (Montclair, NJ: Pooka Publications, 1996).

Milner, Kathleen. *Reiki & Other Rays of Touch Healing* (Privately Published, 1993).

Montgomery, Ruth. *Born to Heal* (New York: Fawcett Books Group, 1985).

Myss, Caroline, Ph.D. *Anatomy of the Spirit* (New York: Harmony Books, 1966).

Paulson, Genevieve Lewis. *Kundalini and the Chakras: A Practical Manual* (St. Paul, MN: Llewellyn Publications, 1997).

Selby, John. *Kundalini Awakening: A Gentle Guide to Chakra Activation and Spiritual Growth* (New York: Bantam Books, 1992).

Shorter, Edward. *From the Mind into the Body* (New York: The Free Press, 1994).

Talbot, Michael. *The Holographic Universe* (New York: HarperPerennial, 1991).

Woolger, Roger J., Ph.D. *Other Lives, Other Selves: A Jungian Psychotherapist Discovers Past Lives* (New York: Bantam Books, 1988).

Zolar. *Dancing Heart to Heart: The Story of Ro-Hun* (McCaysville, GA: Editions Soliel, 1991).

Glossary

The definitions below are given in the context used in this book. They reflect my current level of understanding regarding the way humans are constructed energetically, and the way we interact with others and with the higher dimensions of our reality.

AHMA: American Holistic Medical Association. An association primarily for holistic medical physicians.

AHNA: American Holistic Nurses' Association. An association primarily for holistic nurses and professional caregivers.

Akashic Records: See **Collective Unconscious**

Allopathic Medicine: Traditional form of medical therapy which concentrates on drugs and/or surgery to treat a patient's symptoms.

Alternative Medical Therapies: Holistic approaches or other non-medical methods of addressing a person's entire being: physically, emotionally, mentally, and spiritually. Alternative Therapies include natural foods and herbs, energy-based healing techniques, and movement and meditation techniques such as Tai Chi, Qi Gong, Yoga, etc.

Attunement: In Reiki, an initiation process whereby certain chakras are energetically opened to be better able to receive healing energy. The

153

hand chakras are also opened to transmit these energies through the healer to the client. During the attunement process, the energy of certain symbols is also placed into these chakras. An attunement can only be performed by a Reiki Master (Level III).

Aura: The energy field which surrounds the human physical body. It is composed of several overlapping and interpenetrating energy bodies: the Etheric Body, the Emotional Body, the Mental Body, and the Spiritual Body.

Awareness: See **Consciousness**

Base Chakra: See **Root Chakra**

Block: See **Energy Block**

Brow Chakra: The sixth chakra, located on the forehead midway between the eyes and just above the eyebrow line. Has to do with clarity and insight, both with the physical eyes and with one's inner vision.

Caged One Series: See "**Shadow Self Series**"

Card Session: In Ro-Hun, a process of locating and completely releasing the single most important negative emotional issue the client is facing at that time. Ro-Hun card sessions usually last about an hour, and are conducted with the therapist and the client sitting next to each other.

Chakra (Major): The seven major energy centers located along the front and back of the body; these are most commonly used to describe the human chakra system. They are: (1) Root Chakra, (2) Sacral Chakra (sometimes called the Spleen Chakra), (3) Solar Plexus Chakra, (4) Heart Chakra, (5) Throat Chakra, (6) Brow Chakra (sometimes called the Ajna Chakra or the Third Eye), and (7) the Crown Chakra. See Figure 1 in chapter 1.

Chakra (Minor): The lesser energy centers associated with each joint, palms of the hands, fingertips, soles of the feet, and ends of the toes. These Minor Chakras are characterized by a "spike" of energy extending several inches from the body, as opposed to the spinning vortex which is characteristic of the Major Chakras.

Chi: Chinese word for Life Force Energy that animates all living things: human, animal, and plant.

Clairaudience: The ability to receive guidance and information with your inner hearing. Information received clairaudiently sounds as if someone has spoken the information to you.

Clairsentience: The ability to receive guidance and information in such a way that you simply know it is true. Information received clairsentiently feels like it has the good feeling of truth, and is usually felt in the solar plexus area.

Clairvoyance: The ability to receive guidance and information with your inner vision. Information received clairvoyantly is usually perceived as something that you see, such as a picture, symbol, video clip, or colors/shapes with a particular meaning to you.

Cleanse Session: In Ro-Hun, a single table session (2 to 2½ hours) designed to identify and release emotional issues related to the client's parents; also releases client's feelings of unworthiness, fearfulness, helplessness, and of being too critical or judgmental of self or others. See chapter 4.

Client: A person who comes to an alternative therapy practitioner (who is not a medical doctor) for purposes of returning to health on all levels. Doctors have patients; healers have clients.

Collective Unconscious: A term originated by renowned psychiatrist Carl G. Jung to describe the universal storehouse of memories, "the unwritten history of mankind for time unrecorded," also known as Edgar Cayce's "Akashic Records." The vibrational patterns of the Collective Unconscious contain the record of every thought, word, and deed of every soul who has ever inhabited the earth plane. This information is available to us under the right circumstances.

Complementary Medicine: See **Integrative Medicine**

Conscious Mind: The personality, ego, and intellect associated with an individual person.

Consciousness: The quality of knowing one's own Self as separate from other individual Selves, yet also knowing that on a higher level, all the individually created Selves are but a part of the whole (the Creator) where there is no separation.

Crown Chakra: The seventh major chakra, located at the top of the head. Has to do with the upper brain and higher consciousness.

Disease: A condition where one or more of a person's energy bodies has a disturbance which prevents smooth, harmonious energy vibrations and patterns within those bodies or between adjacent energy bodies. When this nonharmonious vibration pattern is transmitted down into the physical body, it may manifest as pain, improper functioning of organs, or other physical symptoms.

Dowsing: Procedure of placing a pendulum into the spinning vortex of one of the major chakras for the purpose of determining the energy state of that chakra. See chapter 1.

Emotional Body: The second subtle energy body surrounding and interpenetrating the physical body. This body contains the vibrational energy patterns of both our positive and negative emotional reactions to the thought patterns and belief systems contained in the Mental Body.

Energy: The fundamental component of creation which can be expressed as light energy, kinetic (movement) energy, chemical energy, nuclear energy, etc. Energy and matter are interchangeable ($E=mc^2$); therefore, all we see as matter, including ourselves, is a specific form of vibrating energy.

Energy Block: An area on the physical body or in one of the body's energy fields where the vibrational pattern of energy has been disrupted or distorted from its original, natural pattern of perfect health.

Energy Bodies: The subtle energetic layers of our aura which overlap each other and interpenetrate the physical body. Barbara Brennan (in *Hands of Light*) has identified seven energy bodies associated with the physical body: the Etheric, Emotional, Mental, Astral, Etheric Template, Celestial, and Ketheric Template. For this book, I have combined her four higher layers into what I call the Spiritual Body.

Energy Manipulation: Conscious hand movements and intentions to "stir up" suppressed memory patterns in a client's energy field so that these memories can be confronted, dealt with, and released (See chapter 4, "Ro-Hun"). Also a specific set of hand movements to repattern a client's energy field for better functioning on all levels (See chapter 2, "Healing Touch").

Energy Meridians: Pathways within the human body which energetically interconnect chakras, organs, and specific areas of the physical body. Used primarily for acupuncture, acupressure, and other forms of bodywork to move the life-force energy within us.

Energy Modulation: See **Energy Manipulation**

Etheric Body: The first subtle energy body surrounding and interpenetrating the physical body. This body consists of an energy gridwork that forms the template and building instructions for the physical body. The blueprint for every cell and tissue of the physical body is first formed on this energy gridwork.

Faulty Thought: A thought or belief system which, if subscribed to, limits an individual's full, uplifting expression as a confident, secure, and loving human being. Faulty belief systems include: "If you don't believe in my form of religion, you can't go to heaven" and "Human beings just aren't capable of unconditional love." Faulty thoughts include "I am unworthy of abundance" and "I must control others to protect myself."

Foundation Series: In Reiki, the basic series of hand positions which begin each traditional Reiki session.

Golden Rule: "Do unto others as you would have them do unto you." See **Law of Cause and Effect**

Ground (the client): Return the client to full conscious awareness.

Healer: One who facilitates the healing processes of another person. It is important to know that no one can heal another person, but a "healer" can greatly accelerate another person's own internal healing processes. The degree to which healing occurs is determined by the intentions and willingness of both the healer and the client to work together for the client's highest and best good. See chapter 1, "Taking Responsibility for Healing."

Healing Touch: A holistic energy-based program to align and balance the human energy system through many separate healing techniques that include both physical touch and energy field manipulation. See chapter 2, "Healing Touch."

Healing Touch for Animals: A subprogram within Healing Touch that uses specially developed physical and energy body manipulation techniques to restore the health of large and small animals. See chapter 2, "Healing Touch for Animals."

Healing Touch Spiritual Ministry: A subprogram with Healing Touch for ministers, nurses and lay practitioners to provide energy-based healing and laying-on of hands training and education from the perspective of Judaeo-Christian teachings. See chapter 2, "Healing Touch Spiritual Ministry (HTSM)."

Health: A state of original, natural, and harmonious vibration on and among each energetic level of our being. This is very different from "a lack of symptoms or disease."

Heart Chakra: The fourth chakra, located in the center of the chest on a line between the nipples. Has to do with universal love, balance in all things, and healing.

High Heart: In Healing Touch, the energy center in the middle of the breastbone directly above the thymus gland, approximately midway between the Heart and Throat Chakras.

Higher Self: That part of your being which tells you only the Truth, which has only your highest and best interests at heart, and which always loves you unconditionally.

Higher Sense Perception: A term coined by Barbara Brennan (in *Hands of Light*) to mean "a way of perceiving things beyond the normal ranges of human senses." HSP includes clairaudience, clairvoyance, and clairsentience.

Holistic: Addressing all levels of a person's being: physical, emotional, mental, and spiritual. Holistic healing techniques are also concerned with a person's diet, medical treatments, exercise programs, habits such as smoking and overeating, and stress reduction techniques such as meditation or Tai Chi.

Human Energy Field (HEF): That part of the Universal Energy Field which is associated with a particular human being. It consists of the several subtle energy bodies surrounding the physical body, as well as the chakra and meridian systems within the body.

Hypnosis: An artificially induced state of relaxation, in which the subconscious mind is open to various kinds of suggestion, including the vivid recall of lost memories.

Hypnotherapy: A form of psychotherapy that directly or indirectly induces a relaxed hypnotic state in order to gain access to subconscious conflicts and buried traumas, and to alleviate those conditions.

Induction: The process of hypnotically relaxing a person into an altered state for the purpose of gaining access to that person's subconscious mind.

Integrative Medicine: The blending together of allopathic and alternative healing techniques into a truly holistic process for the purpose of preventing disease and, when necessary, restoring a person's original, natural state of perfect health on all levels: physically, emotionally, mentally, and spiritually.

Intuition: That natural ability, developed to varying degrees within each person, that lets us see, feel, and hear with our inner senses.

Karma: The concept that our every thought, word, and action is eventually returned to us in kind. See **Law of Cause and Effect**

Ki: Japanese word for Life Force Energy that animates all living things, human, animal, and plant. See **Chi**

Law of Attraction: One of the fundamental principles upon which our universe is based, which states that we attract people, situations, and opportunities that "resonate with" or that are similar to the vibrational energies that we project from our own Human Energy Field.

Law of Cause and Effect: One of the fundamental principles upon which our universe is based, which states that we must also experience the effect of the experiences we cause. This is done so that, with the knowledge of both sides of a particular action, more enlightened choices can then be made at a soul level to influence future actions. "Do unto others what you would have them do unto you." "Whatsoever a man soweth, so that shall he also reap." "What goes around, comes around."

Law of Duality: One of the fundamental principles upon which our physical universe is based, which states that all of physical creation is expressed in terms of a dual nature: good/bad, black/white, male/female, up/down, light/dark, in/out, here/there, pain/pleasure, etc.

Law of Free Will: One of the fundamental principles upon which our universe is based, which states that The Creator will not interfere with the right of each Spirit to choose for itself what it wants to express. Each Spirit can use this freedom for its own growth or its own limitation.

Light Energization: An energy-based healing technique developed by Mauricio Panisset, a Brazilian healer, which assists in the activation of a person's kundalini energies and energization of the Spiritual Body. See chapter 5.

Magnetic Healing: A general term for healing techniques which focus on healing the etheric body, which is primarily magnetic in nature, as opposed to the physical body, which is primarily electrical in nature.

Mental Body: The third subtle energy body surrounding and interpenetrating the physical body. This body contains the vibrational patterns of all our belief systems and each individual thought associated with our entire soul record.

Meridians: See **Energy Meridians**

Mind: The cognitive, analytical, and creative faculties that work through the ego personality to express a person's desires, wishes, and thoughts.

Past Experience: A life experience that occurred in the past.

Past Life: A lifetime experience which occurred prior to one's current lifetime.

Patient: A person who is under the care of or is being treated by a licensed practitioner or physician.

Pendulum: A small object suspended on a string or thread a few inches long, and is used for dowsing a person's energy field or chakras. It is used as a visible indicator of the interaction of the healer's and client's energy fields. See chapter 1, "Dowsing with a Pendulum."

Physical Body: The vibrational pattern of energy which we recognize by feel, sight, touch, etc. to be our "self." The physical body is also the vehicle we use in this three-dimensional world to express our individual essence. The physical body is built cell by cell upon the pre-existing vibrational pattern of the etheric body.

Prana: Indian word for the Life Force Energy that animates all living things: human, animal, and plant. See **Chi**

Psychiatry: The branch of medicine concerned with psychological illness, especially psychosis, which regards many such abnormalities as organic in origin and which commonly prefers drug treatment to other forms of psychotherapy.

Psychotherapy: A very general term covering many kinds of treatment for psychological disturbances; it may refer to verbal therapies (e.g., psychoanalysis, Jungian analysis), experiential and expressive therapies (e.g., psychodrama), or body-oriented therapies (e.g., Reichian therapy), as well as behavior therapy and psychiatric drug treatment.

Purification Series: In Ro-Hun, a series of three or four table sessions designed to locate, deal with, and completely release all the major victim emotional issues which are holding the client back from expressing his or her full potential.

Reactive Self: In Ro-Hun, the negative emotional energy which is the reaction to a faulty or limiting thought or belief. For example, if you believe the thought, "I am unworthy of abundance," you may react to that thought with a feeling of helplessness. The Reactive Self would then be the Helpless Self, that part of your personality which feels the helplessness.

Reflective Healing: An advanced energy-based healing technique for repatterning the etheric body to its original, natural, and healthy state of being. See chapter 3.

Regression Therapy: A form of hypnotherapy which focuses on the effects of subconscious and previous memories (including past lives) as a means to understanding and releasing emotional blocks.

Reiki: A form of healing that was given to Buddha upon his enlightenment about 2,500 years ago. Reiki healing energy is transmitted through the healer to the client in a form of laying-on of hands. See chapter 2, page 46, "Reiki."

Reincarnation: The belief that, after death, that person's immortal soul will return in another human physical body. The purpose of this process is so that the soul can continue to learn and grow through the choices it makes during the time it is expressed on the earth plane. Eventually, when sufficient growth has occurred and the karmic slate is cleared, the soul can then choose to not reincarnate (return to the earth plane), but instead to continue its spiritual growth in the higher dimensions. Alternatively, it may choose to again return to earth to serve in the instruction and enlightenment of others.

Ro-Hun: A very rapid-acting and life-transforming form of emotional healing that incorporates hypnotherapeutic and energy manipulation techniques to repattern primarily the mental and emotional bodies to a higher level of functioning. See chapter 4.

Root Chakra: The first major chakra, located on the front of the body behind the pubic bone. Has to do with survival and security, the "fight-or-flight" syndrome, and your willingness to be fully present in the world.

Sacral Chakra: The second major chakra, located on the front of the body an inch or two below the navel. Has to do with creativity and relationships, and how you feel about yourself and others.

Scanning: Movement of the hand or fingers through a client's energy field for the purpose of sensing where areas of energy blockages occur.

Shadow Self Series: In Ro-Hun, a series of four table sessions (each 2 to 2½ hours in length) which releases one's abuser/abusive energies. Sometimes called the "Caged One Series."

Skim Session: In Ro-Hun, a single table session which allows the client to release the negative mental and emotional patterns associated with his or her parents, and to release feelings of unworthiness, fearfulness, helplessness, and harsh judgment of self and others. See chapter 4.

Solar Plexus Chakra: The third major chakra, located on the front of the body a few inches above the navel. Has to do with expansiveness, personal power and achievement, and control over your life and the life of others.

Soul: The "personality of the spirit," as opposed to ego, the personality of the physical being. A soul may be advanced (enlightened) or retarded (not enlightened), depending on its choices of how it expresses itself when incarnated on the earth plane.

Soul Record: The accumulated record and vibrational patterns of all beliefs, thoughts, words, and deeds of a single soul throughout the entire history of all its earthly incarnations. As more and more enlightened choices are made while incarnated, the soul record replaces limiting beliefs with positive beliefs; harsh and angry thoughts are replaced with kind and loving thoughts. When all negative vibrations have been replaced as a result of deliberate choice, the karmic balance sheet is cleared and that soul can then choose whether or not to return to the earth plane.

Spirit: An individual essence or spark of life that was created as a spiritual being in the image of the Creator, and which is aware of its own individuality.

Spiritual Body: The fourth subtle energy body surrounding and interpenetrating the physical body. This body contains all of a person's vibrational patterns above the mental octave, and reflects our gestalt consciousness of all that has been learned and experienced by the soul.

Spiritual Healing: A general term for healing techniques that focus on healing the Spiritual Body. See chapter 5.

Spleen Chakra: See **Sacral Chakra**

Subconscious Mind: That part of the psyche that is below the threshold of physical awareness. It has direct access to all aspects of the person's soul record, and under the right circumstances, it also has access to the entire Collective Unconscious.

Subtle: Unseen, as in "Subtle Energy Body."

Synthesized: "The combining of often diverse conceptions into a coherent whole." (Webster's Ninth New Collegiate Dictionary, 1985)

Therapeutic Touch: An energy-based healing technique developed by Delores Kreiger and Dora Kunz to modulate a person's energy field in such a way that physical healing is significantly accelerated. This technique is one of the many techniques taught within the Healing Touch program.

Throat Chakra: The sixth major chakra, located on the front of the body in the throat area where the collarbones come together. Has to do with abundance, expressiveness, and how you view yourself and others.

Universal Energy Field (UEF): The universal energy field consisting of Life Force Energy which permeates all space and animates the process of life. The UEF contains a wide range of vibrational frequencies that are always associated with some form of consciousness, ranging from highly developed to very primitive. The UEF exists in more than three dimensions and is synergistic in nature in that it builds form, rather than contributing to the decay of form (according to Brennan in *Hands of Light*).

Universal Laws: The basic Truths and principles that govern the expression of all life in this universe. These include the Laws of **Attraction, Cause and Effect, Duality,** and **Free Will.**

Womb Experience: The set of experiences, feelings, and beliefs taken on by a fetus from the moment of conception through the moment of birth.

Index

REACH FOR THE MOON

Llewellyn publishes hundreds of books on your favorite subjects! To get these exciting books, including the ones on the following pages, check your local bookstore or order them directly from Llewellyn.

ORDER BY PHONE
- Call toll-free within the U.S. and Canada, 1-800-THE MOON
- In Minnesota, call (651) 291-1970
- We accept VISA, MasterCard, and American Express

ORDER BY MAIL
- Send the full price of your order (MN residents add 7% sales tax) in U.S. funds, plus postage & handling to:

    Llewellyn Worldwide
    P.O. Box 64383, Dept. K055-8
    St. Paul, MN 55164–0383, U.S.A.

POSTAGE & HANDLING
(For the U.S., Canada, and Mexico)
- $4.00 for orders $15.00 and under
- $5.00 for orders over $15.00
- No charge for orders over $100.00

We ship UPS in the continental United States. We ship standard mail to P.O. boxes. Orders shipped to Alaska, Hawaii, The Virgin Islands, and Puerto Rico are sent first-class mail. Orders shipped to Canada and Mexico are sent surface mail.

International orders: Airmail—add freight equal to price of each book to the total price of order, plus $5.00 for each non-book item (audio tapes, etc.).

Surface mail—Add $1.00 per item.

Allow 2 weeks for delivery on all orders.
Postage and handling rates subject to change.

DISCOUNTS
We offer a 20% discount to group leaders or agents. You must order a minimum of 5 copies of the same book to get our special quantity price.

FREE CATALOG
Get a free copy of our color catalog, ***New Worlds of Mind and Spirit***. Subscribe for just $10.00 in the United States and Canada ($30.00 overseas, airmail). Many bookstores carry **New Worlds**—ask for it!

Visit our website at www.llewellyn.com for more information.

The Energy Body Connection

The Healing Experience of Self-Embodiment

Pamela Welch, M.A.

Illness, unresolved emotional issues, and mental patterns that no longer serve you are actually coded messages from your own soul. *The Energy Body Connection* teaches you the truth about these major soul imprints and shows you how to break the code!

This embodiment process acknowledges emotions and physical problems as signposts of transformation. Instead of denying them, you can restructure their energy patterns, awakening your body's cells and tissues through the infusion of a spiritual presence.

Powerful exercises in each chapter help you to discover the meaning of your essential soul patterns, experience your chakra energy centers, direct your consciousness to obtain the results you desire, listen to your body's wisdom, access the healing messages contained in your dreams, work with healing light and color, and meet your spirit guides.

1-56718-819-2, 6 x 9, 360 pp. **$14.95**

Chakras for Beginners

A Guide to Balancing Your Chakra Energies

David Pond

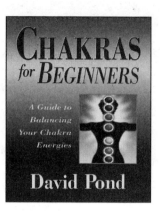

The chakras are spinning vortexes of energy located just in front of your spine and positioned from the tailbone to the crown of the head. They are a map of your inner world—your relationship to yourself and how you experience energy. They are also the batteries for the various levels of your life energy. The freedom with which energy can flow back and forth between you and the universe correlates directly to your total health and well-being.

Blocks or restrictions in this energy flow expresses itself as disease, discomfort, lack of energy, fear, or an emotional imbalance. By acquainting yourself with the chakra system, how they work and how they should operate optimally, you can perceive your own blocks and restrictions and develop guidelines for relieving entanglements.

The chakras stand out as the most useful model for you to identify how your energy is expressing itself. With *Chakras for Beginners* you will discover what is causing any imbalances, how to bring your energies back into alignment, and how to achieve higher levels of consciousness.

1-56718-537-1, 5 ³/₁₆ x 8, 216 pp.   **$9.95**